M000118266

AXIS OF TROUBLE

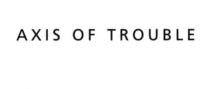

AXIS
OF
TROUBLE

A TROUBLETOWN BOOK

Axis of Trouble
© 2003 by Lloyd Dangle.

For more information:
Lloyd Dangle
Troubletown
P.O. Box 21097
Oakland, CA 94620

ISBN 0-9723544-0-9

5 4 3 2 1

www.troubletown.com

Cover and page design:
Spike Lomibao
johnlomibaodesign.com

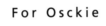

For Osckie

CONTENTS

1   Vortex of Vulgarity

17   Navel of Nefariousness

33   Prism of Partisan Priapism

53   Rhombus of the Ridiculous

67   Bell Curve of Bellicosity

83   Contrapose of Contentedness

97   Tetrahedron of Terror

VORTEX OF VULGARITY

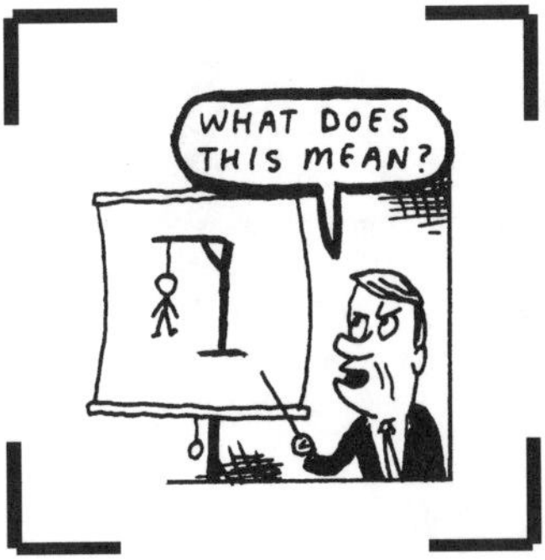
WHAT DOES THIS MEAN?

TROUBLETOWN

BY LLOYD DANGLE

GUILTY

WOO HOOO!

YES!

HEY, HOW ABOUT THAT DOG MAULING CASE, HUH?

THAT WAS A PISSER.

WITH BUTT-UGLY DEFENDANTS LIKE THAT, YOU'VE GOTTA GO WITH THE INSANITY DEFENSE.

NO DOUBT.

SPEAKING OF WHICH, DID YOU CHECK OUT THE SATAN-WOMAN TRIAL IN TEXAS?

BIZARRE!

WHAT'S WITH THE JUDGE ERECTING A BARRIER FOR THE TV CAMERAS?!

THAT JUDGE IS A CLOWN!

YOU SAID IT! WHAT ABOUT THE JUDGE IN ABNER LOUIMA? USELESS!

DON'T REMIND ME! I OWE RICKY $40!

DON'T TELL ME— WHEN ARE YOU GOING TO LEARN NOT TO BET ON COP CONVICTIONS?

I WAS FEELING LUCKY AFTER THE PRIEST WENT DOWN ON MOLESTATION CHARGES.

DO YOU GUYS MIND IF WE WATCH EXTREME GALACTIC WRESTLING?

NO. GO AHEAD AND CHANGE IT.

VULGAR CARTOONISH ENTERTAINMENT.

TROUBLETOWN

DISGUSTING! SO MANY WOMEN ARE GETTING BREAST IMPLANTS NOW PEOPLE THINK IT'S NORMAL!

LOOK! I'LL BET MOST MEN DON'T EVEN KNOW WHAT REAL BREASTS LOOK LIKE!

DON'T BE RIDICULOUS!

IF THERE'S ONE THING MEN ARE SOPHISTICATED ABOUT, IT'S BREASTS!

YOU GIVE MEN TOO MUCH CREDIT.

STRAIGHT MEN AND DRAG QUEENS ALIKE!

OF COURSE WE CAN TELL THE DIFFERENCE! THE FAKE BREASTS LOOK LIKE CANTELOUPES WITH SKIN STRETCHED OVER THEM!

THE WEIRD THING IS, WHY WOULD SO MANY PEOPLE GO FOR CLOWN BOOBS? THEY MUST REALLY THINK IT'S DESIRABLE!

SEE? YOU CAME BACK AROUND TO MY POSITION!

TROUBLETOWN

BY LLOYD DANGLE

"I'D LIKE TO TOAST MY NEW DAUGHTER-IN-LAW AND WARN HER, OUR FAMILY IS JUST LIKE THE SHOW, "SURVIVOR!""

HA! HA! HA! HA! HA! HA! HA!

"WELCOME TO THE "TRIBUNAL," GEORGE!"

HA! HA HA! HA!

HEE HEE!

"FRIENDS, WE'RE GATHERED HERE BECAUSE HUGH WAS "VOTED OFF THE ISLAND" OF LIFE!"

HA! HA! HA! HA! HA! HA!

"MY EX-HUSBAND WAS SO "RICHARD.""

"YOU'RE BEING TERMINATED BECAUSE PEOPLE HERE FEEL YOU DID TOO MUCH FRONTING, LIKE KELLY ON THE SHOW, "BIG BROTHER.""

"PHIL DOESN'T WATCH TELEVISION SO HE MUST BE EATEN."

TROUBLETOWN

HISTORICAL INDICATORS

BY LOLYD DANGLE

OPRAH CANCELLED HER BOOK CLUB.  "THERE AREN'T ENOUGH GOOD BOOKS OUT THERE." *PAF!*	PUBLISHING DECLINED. A-LIST WRITERS WENT HUNGRY; B-LIST WRITERS PERISHED! 	LIBRARIES AND UNIVERSITIES SHUT DOWN.  "WHY BOTHER?!" CLOSED
ABC TOOK TED KOPPEL OFF THE AIR AND REPLACES NIGHTLINE WITH RERUNS OF COPS.  "OUR NEW LINE UP!" • HEE HAW • HOGAN'S HEROES • COPS • BAY W...	WITHOUT KOPPEL, CITIZENS STOP ALL PARTICIPATION IN DEMOCRACY!  "NO THANK YOU. I DON'T NEED TO BUY ANY POLES TODAY." POLLING PLACE	GEORGE R. BUSH BECOMES PRESIDENT BECAUSE OF NAME RECOGNITION.  "AND I ONLY HAVE HALF THE I.Q. OF MY COUSIN DUBYA!"
BILL MOYERS CAN'T FIND WORK ANYWHERE.  ZZZZ IDEAS 35¢	RESTAURANT MENUS ARE PRINTED WITH PICTURES SO THAT PEOPLE DON'T STARVE. "GO DOG GO" IS REMOVED FROM THE LITERARY CANON.  "QUACK?"	AND FOR 800 LONG YEARS, THE WORLD EXPERIENCES A RETURN TO THE DARK AGES.  "I WANT TO WATCH THE SHOPPING CHANNEL!" "I FORGET HOW TO USE THE TV."

TROUBLETOWN

BY LLOYD DANGLE

IT'S THE SHOW WHERE REAL PEOPLE GET SICK AND THROW UP!

RIGHT ON!

DO IT!

HEH!

TONIGHT, REAL PEOPLE WILL PUT LIVE MAGGOTS IN THEIR MOUTHS!

I HEARD ABOUT THIS!

COOL!

WATCH PATHETICALLY DUMB PEOPLE FAIL TO ANSWER EASY QUESTIONS FOR MONEY!

HA! HA! HA! HOW STUPID!

HA! HA!

DESPERATE REAL UGLY PEOPLE ARE LOCKED IN A BAR UNTIL TWO OF THEM HAVE SEX!

OH, -YEAH!

BABY!

SIX PEOPLE ARE MADE TO WORK IN AN OFFICE WHERE THE BOSS IS A SEXUAL PREDATOR!

I LOVE IT!

HEE! HEE!

MEN ARE CONFRONTED BY THEIR WIVES FOR HAVING SEX WITH WOMEN PLANTED ON THE SHOW!

HA HA!

YES!

NOW, A REAL FAMILY OF CHRONIC TV WATCHERS HAS BEEN SECRETLY SELECTED AND TELEVISED THEMSELVES!

COULD IT BE US?!

THE FARBER CHILDREN ARE FORCED TO EAT RAT'S BRAINS WHILE DAD SCREWS THE MAID!

THAT'S NOT US!

I'D HAVE DONE ANYTHING TO BE ON THAT SHOW!

23 MILLION VIEWERS.

I'M GOING TO NEED A DOUBLE DOSE OF RITALIN.

TROUBLETOWN

9 REQUIREMENTS FOR BEING A PUBLIC DEFENDER IN **TEXAS!** / BY LLOYD DANGLE

YOUR SNORING MUST NOT BE SO LOUD THAT IT DROWNS OUT THE PROSECUTOR'S REMARKS

IN COURT, YOUR TALL-BOY MUST BE CONCEALED IN A BROWN BAG AT ALL TIMES.

YOU MUST BE ABLE TO TELL THE DIFFERENCE BETWEEN A BIBLE AND A FEATHER PILLOW.

YOU MUST HAVE THE COGNITIVE SKILLS TO RECOGNIZE YOUR CLIENT.

YOU CAN TRUST ME, RICKY, I'M YOUR ATTORNEY.

YOUR BELT BUCKLE MUST MEET TEXAS STANDARDS FOR SIZE AND DIMENSION.

G'MORNING, COUNSELOR!

YOU MUST PASS THE TEXAS BAR EXAM.

WHAT DOES THIS MEAN?

YOU MUST WORK WELL WITH KIDS AND THE DISABLED.

HEY, LOOK! I'M A PLANE!

YOUR ATTENTION SPAN MUST MEET THE STATE MINIMUM — SET BY THE GOVERNOR!

THREE MINUTES, THAT'S COMMENDABABLE.

YOU MUST EXHIBIT ENOUGH JURISPRUDENCE TO KNOW WHEN YOUR CLIENT IS DEAD.

OBJECTION, YOUR HONOR!

TROUBLETOWN

BY LLOYD DANGLE

BY SUING NAPSTER, THE BAND METALLICA RILED ITS FANS!

REAL ANARCHISTS WOULD GIVE AWAY THEIR MUSIC FOR FREE!

MAKING ME SPEND MY ALLOWANCE IS A BOGUS ACT!

MANY INTERNET GURUS AGREED.

SOON, THE CONCEPT OF "OWNING" A STORY, CARTOON, OR VIDEO WILL BE AS MEANINGLESS AS "MILKING A COW" OR "HAVING SEX WITH ANOTHER PERSON" IS TO ME NOW.

TODAY IS THE NOW

DOWN-LOADING

COPY CAT

IN THEIR VISION OF THE FUTURE, TECHNOLOGY SHOULD DETERMINE OUR CUSTOMS, LAWS, AND VALUES.

THIS DEVICE ENABLES ME TO STEAL CARS!

WELL THEN AUTO THEFT MUST NOT BE A CRIME.

IN THE VIRTUAL COMMUNITY, A FEW WILL SACRIFICE FOR THE BENEFIT OF FREE ENTERTAINMENT FOR ALL!

MOTHER, I'VE TAKEN A VOW TO BECOME A WEB ANIMATOR.

A MARTYR!

SOB! SOB!

NOW NOT 44!

COMPUTERS AND SOFTWARE WILL STILL COST PLENTY, HOWEVER, AND PENALTIES FOR UNAUTHORIZED USE WILL BE SEVERE!

I PIRATED MY mom'S COPY OF QUICKBOOKS PRO.

I USED THE WORD "WINDOWS" IN MY CARPENTRY BUSINESS.

WITHOUT THE ECONOMIC INCENTIVE, MONEYGRUBBERS LIKE METALLICA WILL FIND OTHER JOBS. THANKFULLY YOU'LL STILL BE ABLE TO LISTEN TO NEIL YOUNG!

I'LL LET THE RECORD LABEL WORRY ABOUT THE MONEY; I'LL WORRY ABOUT WARBLING LIKE AN OLD GOOSE!

TROUBLETOWN

BY LLOYD DANGLE

Panel 1: WHEN A RECORD COMPANY "SIGNS" A BAND, IT'S AN EVIL TRANSACTION.

SIGN OVER ALL RIGHTS OF AUTHORSHIP TO YOUR MUSIC AND WE'LL GIVE YOU A GOLD LEXUS!

HEH!

YEAH, momma!

HEH!

HEH! HEH! SUCKER!

Panel 2: THAT'S WHY YOU ALWAYS HEAR ABOUT MUSICIANS BEING SCREWED OUT OF THEIR OWN CREATIONS.

YOU INFRINGED SCHMENKODISK'S COPYRIGHTED GUITAR RIFF FROM THE SONG "HOOEY HOOEY," THAT YOU WROTE IN 1995!

HAH! HAH!

Panel 3: BUT NOW, ALONG COMES NAPSTER GNUTELLA, AND A HOST OF OTHERS TO **TAKE BACK** THE **MUSIC!**

TAKE THAT, SLIME!

EAT MY SHOE, SCUMBAG.

THWAK!

MM OO!

EAR REBEL .COM

MUSIC HOUND .COM

KICK!

Panel 4: AND THE PEOPLE **LOVE** IT!

WE DESERVE TO HAVE FREE MUSIC BECAUSE PEOPLE LIKE MICK JAGGER ARE TOO RICH!

ANY BAND THAT DOESN'T **SUCK** CAN LIVE MODESTLY OFF THEIR GIGS & T-SHIRTS.

HOOTIE

LIMP BISK!

Panel 5: BUT ANY DAY NOW AT NAPSTER HQ:

THINK SHAWN, WE CAN KEEP SUING YOUR ASS FOR 70 YEARS—OR YOU CAN BECOME VICE PRESIDENT OF NAPSTER-SEAGRAMS-SCHMENKODISK AND DRIVE A GOLD LEXUS!

OOH!

NAPSTER

Panel 6: AND SOON:

AREN'T YOU GOING TO SIGN ME TO A HORRENDOUS WORK FOR HIRE DEAL?

NAH! WE NO LONGER HAVE THAT FORMALITY. WE **STEAL** YOUR MUSIC WITH IMPUNITY NOW.

BUT WE DO TAKE 40% OF YOUR T-SHIRT GROSS.

Everything Must GO!

BACK   FORWARD   RELOAD   STOP   SHOP   UNLOCK   PRINT   SEARCH   HOME

http://www.potatopix.com/deadmeat/bankrupt.htm

Potatopix online e-liquidation!

AS SECURE AS CAN BE EXPECTED UNDER THE CIRCUMSTANCES.

OFFICE TRAMPOLINE (SLIGHTLY WORN)

BOING! $200

ROLODEX FULL OF BASTARDS WHO USED TO GIVE US MONEY.

$2

PLASTIC CHAIRS IN ALL THOSE DAMN imac COLORS.

$13

ONE CEO SIDEBURN TRIMMER

DIGITAL! $10

ONE DRY ERASE BOARD WITH IMPRESSIVE E-STRATEGY DOODLES. $15

PALM PILOT POTPOURRI! (CARDBOARD BOX INCLUDED) $8

NAVEL ORANGES — THIS SIDE UP

OUR BUSINESS PLAN

(CAN DOUBLE AS A COCKTAIL NAPKIN!)

TRENDY LOFT LEASE

DOT LOFTS

EIGHTEEN MONTHS RENT DUE

SCOOTER BRIEFLY RIDDEN BY A GOATEED MILLIONAIRE.

OUR DOMAIN NAME IN DOT-COM, DOT-NET, AND DOT-ORG!

ALL THREE! $45

VENDING MACHINE (CHIPS & CORN NUTS)

$50

ACCEPTS COINS OR OUR COMPANY'S STOCK CERTIFICATES

EVEN THE SOCKET LAYER MUST GO!

MAKE AN OFFER.

TROUBLETOWN

THE OTHER U.N.

BY LLOYD DANGLE

Panel 1: WE ALL AGREE HE IS A MENACE AND A MADMAN! SOMETHING MUST BE DONE!

Panel 2: HE'S THUMBED HIS TINY LITTLE NOSE AT THE ENTERTAINMENT COMMUNITY LONG ENOUGH! IT'S TIME FOR ACTION!

Panel 3: YES, BUT WE MUST WORK THROUGH THE UNITED NETWORKS. ONE SUPERSTATION CANNOT ACT ALONE!

Panel 4: ALRIGHT, WE'LL GIVE THIS INEFFECTUAL BODY 24 HOURS— AFTER THAT WE GO AFTER MICHAEL JACKSON **ALONE!**

Panel 5: OKAY, I'LL LET THE PAPARAZZI SET UP CAMP IN MY FRONT YARD. I'LL GIVE A COMPLETE DISCLOSURE ON THE CONDITION OF MY NOSE!

Panel 6: MICHAEL APPEARS TO BE COOPERATING, OH **COME ON!** IT'S A RUSE! HE'S PLAYING US!

Panel 7: PBS WILL HAVE NO PART OF THIS CHARADE. EFFETE BASTARDS! AFTER ALL WE'VE DONE FOR YOU?

Panel 8: HE HAS **NOT** GIVEN IN TO OUR DEMANDS, I HAVE SPY FOOTAGE THAT SHOWS CHILD PORN ALL OVER THAT HOUSE!

Panel 9: HE USED TO BE OUR CELEBRITY SPOKES-PERSON, BUT IF YOU'RE GOING TO ATTACK, WE'LL ADVERTISE!

TROUBLETOWN

BY LLOYD
DANGLE

PEOPLE ACT LIKE WE'RE SEX SLAVES! DARN IT, THIS IS A CONSENSUAL RELATIONSHIP!

I DID IT TO SHOCK MY PARENTS. I THOUGHT ABOUT BECOMING A STRIPPER BUT I DECIDED TO INTERN INSTEAD!

I WANT TO BE A CORPORATE LOBBYIST, SO IF THIS INTERNSHIP REQUIRES ME TO COMMIT UNSPEAKABLE ACTS— **BRING IT ON!**

DARTMOUTH

'' HEH!'
HEH!

IT'S LIKE THE SAME EPISODE OF WEST WING OVER AND OVER AND OVER!

I HATE IT!

I **WILL** BE PRESIDENT ONE DAY. I **WILL!** EVERY DAY AND EVERY WAY I'M GETTING CLOSER!!

FRANCOS

SEX? NO. I'M LEARNING HOW TO MAKE DOCUMENTS DISAPPEAR!

PLEASE! I HAVE A 4.0 AT STANFORD—I'M NOT GOING TO SLEEP WITH A LOSER WHO ONLY CHAIRS ONE KEY SUB-COMMITTEE!

ORAL SEX WITH SENATOR HUFFENDORF WASN'T FUN, BUT IT'LL LOOK GREAT ON MY RESUME.

YALE

NO. ACTUALLY, SEX WAS THE ONLY COMPROMISE OF MY VALUES I **WASN'T** ASKED TO MAKE!

STORY OF MY LIFE.

TROUBLETOWN

BY LLOYD DANGLE

IN THE ENTERTAINMENT BIZ, WE DEAL WITH CONSTANT ATTEMPTS BY OUTSIDERS TO INTERFERE WITH OUR CONTENT.

OUR PUBLISHER'S DOG JUST HAD PUPPIES! CAN YOU WORK IT INTO THIS WEEK'S STRIP?

IN AREAS OF THE MEDIA WHERE MONEY IS INVOLVED, WE'VE HEARD THE PRESSURE IS EVEN WORSE!

NOT BAD! DO TWO MORE DRAFTS AND I'LL BE READY TO STEAL YOUR SCREENWRITER'S CREDIT.

HOLLYWOOD

ADVERTISERS ARE NO LONGER HAPPY RUNNING ADS IN-BETWEEN THE SHOWS, THEY WANT PLACEMENT.

HOLD STILL, MR. RATHER, WHILE WE DIGITALLY IMPOSE THE KENTUCKY FRIED CHICKEN LOGO ONTO YOUR FOREHEAD.

CBS NEWS

NOW EVEN THE WHITE HOUSE PAYS TO HAVE SCRIPT APPROVAL.

THE ANTI-DRUG MESSAGE IN THIS SCENE IS GOOD, BUT SHOULDN'T TORI SPELLING HAVE HER SHIRT OFF?

YEAH!

THANK GOODNESS THERE ARE STILL A FEW "CREATIVES" WITH ENOUGH INTEGRITY TO RESIST SUCH MANIPULATION.

YOU'LL BE LUCKY TO SELL MUFFINS IN THIS TOWN!

EAT ME! I QUIT!

ON THE OTHER HAND, IT CAN BE NO PROBLEM AT ALL IF IT'S HANDLED WITH SUBTLETY.

CONGRATS ON YOUR PUPS, AKRON WEEKLY!

$20,000

TROUBLETOWN

BY LLOYD DANGLE

"DID YOU HEAR ABOUT BOB KERREY?"

"OF COURSE! COMBAT VETERAN, WAR HERO. HE OUGHTA BE PRESIDENT!"

"I'M SICK OF THESE POLITITIONS WHO SMOKED POT IN COLLEGE DURING THE WAR AND NOW PRETEND TO BE TOUGH!"

"BUT KERREY KILLED INNOCENT WOMEN AND CHILDREN."

"ULP!"

"THAT'S BARBARIC! NO WONDER HE IS SO SELF-REFLECTIVE. THAT'S WHAT THAT'S ALL ABOUT."

"THAT MADE ME SUSPICIOUS!"

"SO DO YOU THINK WE'RE BETTER OFF WITH A POT SMOKING AIR NATIONAL GUARD PRESIDENT?"

"OH, JUST SHUT UP..."

"...AND TRY TO ENJOY THE EXECUTION."

TROUBLETOWN

AXIS OF SCHADENFREUDE

BY LLOYD DANGLE

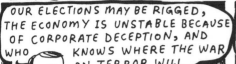

Panel 1: OUR ELECTIONS MAY BE RIGGED, THE ECONOMY IS UNSTABLE BECAUSE OF CORPORATE DECEPTION, AND WHO KNOWS WHERE THE WAR ON TERROR WILL LEAD?!

SECUR — ON

Panel 2: THEY TALK ABOUT AN AXIS OF EVIL, I SAY THERE'S AN **AXIS OF TROUBLE** — AND WE'RE RIGHT IN THE MIDDLE OF IT!

SECU — ON

Panel 3: SCHADENFREUDE.

WHAT WAS THAT YOU SAID?

SCHADENFREUDE, MAN! IT'S THE ONLY THING THAT KEEPS ME GOING!

SECU

Panel 4: IS IT SOME KIND OF GERMAN DESIGNER DRUG? IS THIS A TEST TO SEE IF I'LL REPORT YOU?

NO, SCHADENFREUDE IS THE EUPHORIA THAT COMES FROM OTHER PEOPLE'S MISFORTUNES.

BEEP!

Panel 5: LIKE WHEN A BUSH DAUGHTER GETS BUSTED FOR DRUGS OR MARTHA STEWART GOES DOWN FOR CORRUPTION!

HA HA! YEAH, LIKE WHEN A CELEBRITY ATHLETE IS ARRESTED FOR DRUNK DRIVING?

HA! HA!

EXACTLY! HA!

Panel 6: COME THIS WAY PLEASE.

BUT I'LL MISS MY FLIGHT!

SORRY.

HEH! HEH! HEH!

NAVEL OF
NEFARIOUSNESS

TROUBLETOWN

BY LLOYD DANGLE

I'M ASKING YOU DIRECTLY, DID YOU ENERGY PRODUCERS **GOUGE** THE PEOPLE OF CALIFORNIA?

ENERGY SUBCOMMITTEE

ABSOLUTELY NOT, SIR! I HAVE AN MBA...WHAT WE'RE SEEING IS A LAW OF MARKET ECONOMICS CALLED "OVER THE BARREL BARGAINING."

ALLOW ME TO ILLUSTRATE...

BOSCO ELECTRIC

QUALITY KILOWAT

SUPPOSE YOU WERE BITTEN BY A RATTLESNAKE IN THE DESERT AND I CAME ALONG WITH THE ONLY SNAKEBITE KIT WITHIN 100 MILES...

WHILE THE COST OF MY SNAKEBITE KIT MAY BE ONLY $1.98, THE SUDDEN HIGH DEMAND RAISES ITS MARKET VALUE TO $300 MILLION!

AND, IF I HAPPENED TO KNOW YOU HAD A COUPLE HUNDRED BILLION SURPLUS DOLLARS STASHED AWAY, ITS VALUE WOULD NATURALLY RISE ANOTHER 8000 TO 9000%.

BOSCO ELECTRIC

YOU CAN'T ARGUE WITH SOUND ECONOMIC REASONING! I JUST WISH I OWNED A COUPLE HUNDRED SHARES OF THAT ACTION!

THE SPOT MARKET **ROCKS** SENATOR!

GOOD TIMES!

HA! HA!

TROUBLETOWN

BY LLOYD DANGLE

HALF 'N' HALF AND THE COFFEE WHITENER INDUSTRY HAD FOUGHT LONG & HARD FOR DEREGULATION.

TODAY IS THE DAY!

SENATORS, CREAMER DEREGULATION WILL MEAN MORE CHOICE FOR CONSUMERS. AND COMPETITION WILL BRING LOWER PRICES!

MOCHA MIX

HALF N HALF

SWEET N WHITE

DEMAND WAS AT AN ALL TIME HIGH.

HURRY UP OR I'LL POKE YOUR EYE OUT WITH A STIRRER!

I CAN'T DRINK IT BLACK!

THANKS TO THEIR CONNECTIONS, THE INDUSTRY SOON RECEIVED THE MOST SWEEPING DEREGULATION EVER!

YES! NOW LET'S GET THE HELL OUTTA HERE!

THE NEXT DAY:

SO NOW DO WE DROP OUR PRICES?

NO, YOU IDIOT! NOW WE MUST PRODUCE A SHORTAGE!

AND SO, LIKE GASOLINE, CABLE, TELEPHONE, HEALTH CARE, AND UTILITIES, COFFEE CREAMER BECAME UNAFFORDABLE TO MOST TROUBLETOWNERS.

ELMERS?

CONSERVE IT!

TROUBLETOWN

THIS YEAR'S CORPORATE EXCUSES FOR HIGHER PRICES

BY LLOYD DANGLE

THE POLITICIANS DIDN'T GIVE US THE KIND OF **DEREGULATION** WE PAID 'EM FOR!

THERE'S NOT ENOUGH ALASKAN CRUDE LEFT FOR THE U.S. MARKET. SUPPLY AND DEMAND CAUSED THE INCREASE.

AFTER OUR PROFITS & CEO SALARIES WE'RE PRACTICALLY BANKRUPT! WE SERIOUSLY NEED A BAILOUT!

TOO MANY PEOPLE PUT THEIR SELFISH DESIRE TO AVOID **CANCER** ABOVE THE NEEDS OF THE POWER GRID!

THAT MOVIE, ERIN BROCKOVITCH.

TOO MANY PEOPLE TOOK OUR ADVICE & SWITCHED TO NATURAL GAS ALL AT ONCE.

OF COURSE THE PRICE SKYROCKETED!

RUNNING A MONOPOLY HAS HIDDEN COSTS.

PIPELINE IRREGULARITIES.

DON'T BLAME US BECAUSE YOU PEOPLE CAN'T **CONSERVE**.

TROUBLETOWN

THE CHOKE POINT!

BY LLOYD DANGLE

TROUBLETOWN

BY LLOYD DANGLE

GENERAL SHINSEKI THOUGHT IT WOULD BE A GREAT IDEA FOR EVERY PERSON IN THE ARMY TO WEAR A BLACK BERET.

BUT WE DON'T MANUFACTURE BLACK BERETS IN AMERICA ANYMORE, SO SUPPLY GRUNT PFC. MOOREHEAD HAD TO RELY ON OUR NAFTA AND FTAA TRADE PARTNERS.

BUENAS DÍAS, YO NECESITO...

¿600,000 BERETS EN NEGRO POR FAVOR?

IMPOSIBLE. MI CASA DE PERSPIRACION ES MUY OCUPADA CON LA FABRICACION DE LIZ CLAIBORNE JUNIOR WEAR!

SO HE CALLED OUR MOST FAVORED NATION TRADE PARTNER AND LUCKILY GOT SOMEONE WHO SPOKE ENGLISH.

600,000 BERETS? NO PROBLEM! WE'LL USE DISSIDENTS AND FULAN GONG PRACTITIONERS!

CRANK

CRCK! TORTURE!

THEN WORD CAME DOWN FROM DICK CHENEY: MEN, WE MUST BE PREPARED TO GO TO WAR— WITH THE COMMUNIST DEMONS WHO SEWED OUR HATS.

CHINA

SPEAKING OF THAT WAR...

HELLO, CHINA? I'D LIKE TO ORDER 800,000,000 TONS OF STEEL.

WE'VE GOT THIS BIG WAR TO FIGHT AND WE DON'T PRODUCE IT ANYMORE.

CHINA

TROUBLETOWN

THIS YEAR'S FREE TRADE SIDE AGREEMENTS

BY LLOYD DANGLE

STERN SUGGESTION: DON'T USE FORCED CHILD LABOR ANY MORE THAN IS ABSOLUTELY NECESSARY.

THE PRISONERS HAVE HEPATITIS!

THE FTAA MUST BE FULLY DEMOCRATIC — EXCEPT AT THE PLANNING SUMMITS.

HELLO, FRANZ! ENJOYING QUEBEC?

LOVELY!

REQUEST THAT FACTORIES VOLUNTARILY STOP DUMPING DIOXINS IN THE OPEN WHILE JANE PAULEY'S TV CREW IS PRESENT.

PEOPLE DO!

MEXICO WILL CHANGE ITS NAME.

VIVA! WELCOME TO TEXACO! VIVA!

UNION ORGANIZERS MAY BE TORTURED UPON DETECTION IN ANY FTAA COUNTRY.

MAS CERVEZAS!

INVESTORS CAN SUE LATIN AMERICAN DICTATORS FOR POOR MARKET PERFORMANCE.

YOU PINCHED MY PORTFOLIO, PINOCHET!

AIR HOLES MUST BE PUNCHED IN BOXCARS CARRYING CHATTEL.

COYOTE BRAND HUMAN CARGO

INVESTORS CAN SUE ANY COUNTRY THAT REFUSES TO ENJOY CHEMICAL BYPRODUCTS IN THEIR DRINKING WATER.

FOREIGN CAPITAL HAS RIGHTS TOO!

ANY FOREIGN LEADER WHO ENACTS BARRIFS AND TERRIERS WILL FACE A WAR TRIMES CRIBUNAL.

PARDON MY CHARMING GAFFE!

EL PRESIDE ESTATES UN

HA! HA!

HA!

TROUBLETOWN

BY LLOYD DANGLE

Panel 1: THE GOOD NEWS IS THAT ALL OF THE PEOPLE WHO ENCOUNTERED THE MUTANT MUSHROOMS AT 3-MILE ISLAND HAVE FINALLY DIED.

Panel 2: ALL OF OUR MARKET DATA SHOWS US THAT CONDITIONS ARE RIGHT TO ONCE AGAIN AGGRESSIVELY MARKET NUCLEAR POWER!

Panel 3: YOU'RE SURE NOBODY WHO HAD A RUN-IN WITH ONE OF THOSE MUSHROOMS SURVIVED?

POSITIVE.

THANK GOD!

Panel 4: SO, HERE'S ONE OF OUR CONCEPTS: "WHAT'S A LITTLE CANCER?" A SERIES OF PSA'S TO REMIND PEOPLE THAT EVEN THE SUN CAUSES CANCER!

WHAT'S

Panel 5: I SAW PICTURES OF A KID WHO WAS HALF EATEN BY A CHERNOBYL DANDELION. I COULDN'T EAT RED MEAT FOR A WEEK!

Panel 6: CONSIDER THIS: LET'S PLAY OFF THE NATURALLY SUGGESTIVE SHAPES OF NUCLEAR COOLING TOWERS TO BRAND A HOT NEW SEXY IMAGE.

NUCLEAR MELT DOWN!

Panel 7: SEX LEADS TO BABIES AND WE DON'T WANT PEOPLE THINKING ABOUT BIRTH DEFECTS!

DON'T BE SO LITERAL!

Panel 8: YOU PEOPLE SEEM UNWILLING TO THINK OUTSIDE THE BOX...

I HAVE TO TAKE THIS.

CHIRP! CHIRP!

Panel 9: MECHANICSBURGH, PA! THIS TIME IT'S TUB AND TILE MILDEW ON THE LOOSE!

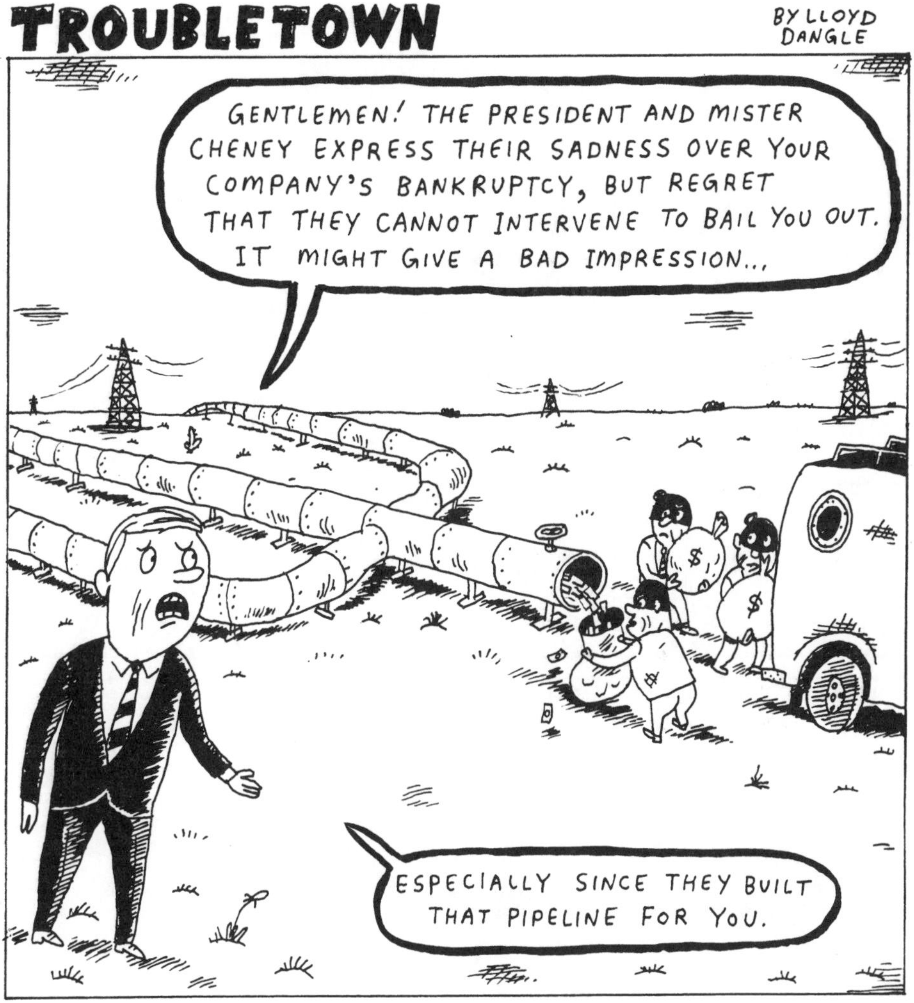
TROUBLETOWN
BY LLOYD DANGLE
GENTLEMEN! THE PRESIDENT AND MISTER CHENEY EXPRESS THEIR SADNESS OVER YOUR COMPANY'S BANKRUPTCY, BUT REGRET THAT THEY CANNOT INTERVENE TO BAIL YOU OUT. IT MIGHT GIVE A BAD IMPRESSION...
ESPECIALLY SINCE THEY BUILT THAT PIPELINE FOR YOU.

TROUBLETOWN

9 SIGNS THAT YOUR BOSS WILL DEEP-SIX THE COMPANY

BY LLOYD DANGLE

HE PAYS YOU A GENEROUS YEAR-END BONUS IN COMPANY STOCK HE'S UNLOADING.

JESUS, I'M GLAD TO GET RID OF, I MEAN, REWARD YOU WITH THIS!

HIS DAUGHTER DRIVES TO HIGH SCHOOL IN A LEXUS PURCHASED WITH YOUR 401(K).

THE OVERSEAS SHAM SUBSIDIARIES START OPENING SHAM SUBSIDIARIES HERE!

HI! JIM REEVES OF OBIE WAN KANOBIE CORP. BOSTON!

$

HE IS SUDDENLY APPOINTED AMBASSA-DOR TO LUXEMBOURG.

IT'S COLDER HERE THAN TEXAS!

HIS MISTRESS TURNS WHISTLEBLOWER!

LET'S SEE YOUR WHISTLE.

$

NONE OF PHIL GRAMM'S FAMILY MEMBERS DRAW AN UNEXPLAINED SALARY ANYMORE.

MICKEY GRAMM   MARGE GRAMM   HUGH GRAMM   RH GR

THE ACCOUNTANT ASKS YOU TO STORE THE COMPANY'S FINANCIAL RECORDS AT YOUR APARTMENT.

DON'T OPEN THE DOOR FOR ANYONE.

NO PARKING

LOADING DOCK

THE SOUTHERN CENTRAL UNITED STATES EXPERIENCES A SUDDEN SHORTAGE OF DOCUMENT SHREDDERS.

SORRY, THE GALVESTON OFFICE MAX IS OUT TOO. I CAN TRY CALLING LUBBOCK.

OFFICE

EVERY MEMBER OF CONGRESS WITHOUT A CONFLICT OF INTEREST APPEARS AT A JOINT PRESS CONFERENCE.

TV 5

TROUBLETOWN

BY LLOYD DANGLE

Panel 1: YOU KNOW, YOU DON'T NEED TO BE A CORPORATE HOTSHOT TO ENJOY ALL THE PERKS AND BENEFITS OF THE ANCIENT ART OF **ACCOUNTING!**

Panel 2: **AUDIT MAGIC** IS THE THE ONLY SOFTWARE PRODUCT THAT PUTS ALL THE TRICKS AND MANEUVERS OF BIG-TIME CORPORATE BOOKKEEPING RIGHT UP **YOUR** SLEEVE!

AUDIT MAGIC WINDOWS

Panel 3: TRANSFER DEBTS INTO ASSETS, TURN LOSSES INTO PROFITS — OR DO IT ALL THE OTHER WAY AROUND! YOU CAN EVEN TURN YOUR IN-LAWS INTO A DUMMY SUBSIDIARY!

THEY'VE GOT THE **DUMMY** PART DOWN ALREADY!

HA! HA! HA!

Panel 4: AUDIT MAGIC WILL CHANGE YOUR LIFE — AND IT'S FULLY CUSTOMIZABLE TO YOUR TOLERANCE FOR RISK AND ADVENTURE!

HOP ON!

AUDIT MAGIC

Panel 5: ONCE YOU'VE MASTERED COOKING THE BOOKS LIKE A **TITAN**, YOU'RE READY FOR OUR OTHER FINE PRODUCTS!

PLEAD THE FIFTH MAGIC!

AVOID EXTRADITION MAGIC 2.0

BANKRUPTCY MAGIC! PRO

FIRE YOUR EMPLOYEES MAGIC! 2.0

#1

Panel 6: **BONUS!** ONCE YOU START BEHAVING LIKE A CEO, YOU'LL NEVER HAVE TO WORRY ABOUT AN **IRS** TAX AUDIT AGAIN!

SHOULD WE AUDIT THIS GUY?

HE HAS **AUDIT MAGIC!** LET'S NAIL THE WAITRESS IN TOPEKA!

IRS IRS

TROUBLETOWN

E-Z GUIDE TO BANKRUPTCY
CORPORATE & PERSONAL

BY LLOYD DANGLE

PEOPLE WHO FILE FOR BANKRUPTCY ARE CONSIDERED DEADBEATS AND SPENDTHRIFTS.  I DON'T HAVE A JOB, SO I BOUGHT A JET SKI!	PEOPLE WHO FILE FOR CORPORATE BANKRUPTCY ARE BRILLIANT STRATEGISTS.  PURE GENIUS. BANKRUPT BILLIONAIRE	YOUR SENATOR WANTS TO SEE BANKRUPT SCHMOES PAYING BACK VISA FOR LIFE.  AT THE HIGHEST INTEREST RATE! VISA EVERYWHERE YOU WANT TO BE!	YOUR SENATOR WANTS TO SEE BANKRUPT CEOS AT HIS NEXT FUNDRAISING DINNER.  CHARMED, I'M SURE!!
PERSONAL BANKRUPTCY MEANS YOU DON'T QUALIFY FOR A MORTGAGE.  SORRY.	CORPORATE BANKRUPTCY MEANS YOU DON'T NEED A MORTGAGE.  I'LL TAKE IT!	PERSONAL BANKRUPTCY IS A SOURCE OF ANGUISH AND SHAME.  WHY? WHY MUST I USE SO MUCH FOOD AND RENT?	CORPORATE BANKRUPTCY IS A BLEMISH ON THE CEO'S RESUME.  CONSIDERING YOUR PREVIOUS BANKRUPTCY, STARTING PAY WILL BE $780 MILLION.
PERSONAL BANKRUPTCIES PUT A DRAG ON THE WHOLE CREDIT CARD SYSTEM.  WE DIDN'T EXPECT THIS TO BE A RISKY BUSINESS! APPLY TODAY $20,000 LIMIT NO QUESTIONS	CORPORATE BANKRUPTCIES ARE ONLY A PROBLEM FOR FIRED EMPLOYEES, SHAREHOLDERS, AND TAXPAYERS.  IT'S HEALTHY IN THE LONG RUN.	CORPORATE BANKRUPTCY MEANS YOU'RE SUITABLE FOR PUBLIC OFFICE.  HECK, WE ALL DID IT BACK THEN!	PERSONAL BANKRUPTCY MEANS YOU'RE SUITABLE FOR **LOTS MORE** CREDIT CARDS! SEEING HOW MUCH DEBT YOU CARRY, I CAME OUT PERSONALLY.

TROUBLETOWN

 BY LLOYD DANGLE

WHAT IF BUSH AND CHENEY KEPT THEIR PROMISE TO RUN THE COUNTRY LIKE A BUSINESS? EFFICIENCY. BOTTOM LINE.

THEY WOULD'VE USED DIRTY ACCOUNTING TRICKS. I CAN GIVE A $1.6 TRILLION TAX CUT, TRIPLE THE MILITARY BUDGET, AND NOT RUN A DEFICIT!

THEY WOULD'VE PAID THEMSELVES CEO SALARIES. THOU DEAR BROTHER, WELCOME TO THE EMIRATE OF FLORIDA! KING JEB!

THEY WOULD SEND DISASTER RELIEF TO FICTICIOUS STATES. TONIGHT **CHENEYTUCKY** IS UNDER A STATE OF EMERGENCY.

THEY WOULD MOVE THE NATION'S CAPITAL TO BERMUDA. IT WAS A DISINCENTIVE TO SERVE IN PUBLIC LIFE— KNOWING YOU WOULD HAVE TO PAY TAXES. MEET THE PRES

THEY WOULD TREAT CITIZENS LIKE THEIR EMPLOYEES. RELAX— THIS IS NO DIFFERENT THAN LOOTING AN EMPLOYEE PENSION FUND! SOCIAL SECURITY

THEY WOULD CHANGE THE NAME OF THE LINCOLN BEDROOM TO THE CHEVRON BEDROOM.

SLEEP BETTER KNOWING YOUR CAR HAS TECHRON

THEY WOULD SHARE INSIDER INFORMATION WITH MARTHA STEWART. PSSST! SELL IRAQI K-MART! BOMBING STARTS TONIGHT!

THEY'D RUN THE COUNTRY INTO THE GROUND AND MAKE OUT LIKE BANDITS! WE WEREN'T AWARE! ARTHUR ANDERSEN DID IT!

29

TROUBLETOWN

BY LLOYD DANGLE

Panel 1:
UH-OH! WORLDCOM WENT BANKRUPT! I'D BETTER FIND A NEW LONG-DISTANCE CARRIER.

DON'T BE RIDICULOUS. YOUR SERVICE WON'T BE AFFECTED.

Panel 2:
I DON'T GET IT, DAD! HOW CAN THE BIGGEST BANKRUPTCY IN HISTORY **NOT** AFFECT THE COMPANY'S SERVICES?

HONESTLY, SON! DON'T BE A SIMPLETON!

Panel 3:
"TELECOMMUNICATIONS" WAS JUST A **CODE WORD**—THE **VEIL** THAT ALLOWED WORLDCOM TO BE A PLAYER! YOU DON'T REALLY THINK **ENRON** WAS PEDDLING THE JUICE FOR YOUR TOASTER OVEN, DO YOU?

WHAT, THEN?

Panel 4:
VALUATIONS OF **NOTHINGNESS**, SON—THE PUREST FORM OF CAPITALISM THERE IS! EVERY FEW YEARS YOU MUST GO BANKRUPT IN ORDER TO TAKE YOUR EARNINGS AND LAUNDER THE MONEY!

?

Panel 5:
DO YOU REMEMBER THE REFINERY FIRE THAT TOOK YOUR MOTHER'S LIFE?

OF COURSE!

SUPPOSE I TOLD YOU THERE **NEVER WAS** A REFINERY, YOUR MOM AND I WERE INTO SOME VERY KINKY ACCOUNTING.

MOM? SHE'S ALIVE.

Panel 6:

THIS CONVERSATION HAS DONE NOTHING TO RESTORE MY INVESTOR CONFIDENCE.

WITH KNOWLEDGE THERE'S PAIN, SON. SAY HELLO TO DOLORES FOR ME.

TROUBLETOWN

BY LLOYD DANGLE

STEVE CASE RESIGNED AS THE CHAIRMAN OF AOL TIME WARNER, THIS IS IT! THIS IS **DEFINITELY** IT!

THE STOCK MARKET HAS HIT **ROCK BOTTOM!** IT'S THE PERFECT TIME TO BUY!

WHO SAYS?

WHO SAYS? UH, ALL THE ANALYSTS, IN-SIDERS, EXPERTS...

THEN I DON'T BELIEVE IT! YOU'RE THE ONES WHO SCREWED ME THE FIRST TIME!

BECAUSE I INVESTED, MY SON CAN'T AFFORD TO ATTEND A STATE COLLEGE!

I'M SO SORRY.

LET ME MAKE IT UP TO YOU. I CAN PUT YOU INTO SOME SHORT-YIELD HIGH-GROWTH LONG BONDS AT AN AMAZING DISCOUNT!

NO THANK YOU!

IF YOU SAW A STORE WITH SIGNS SAYING "**EVERYTHING 90% OFF**," YOU'D GO SHOPPING, WOULDN'T YOU?

ASSUMING I WASN'T PENNILESS.

IN CASE YOU'RE STILL WORRYING ABOUT THE SCANDALS, LOOK, HERE ARE CEOS BEING TAKEN AWAY IN HAND-CUFFS!

I'VE SEEN THAT SAME FOOTAGE 100 TIMES! I BELIEVE THOSE ARE ACTORS! IT'S A SCAM AND I'M NOT BUYING IT!

5 MINUTES LATER AT AN ARMY RECRUITING OFFICE:

THERE'S A GOOD CHANCE YOU'LL NEVER SEE ACTIVE DUTY, AND "GULF WAR SYNDROME" WON'T BE A PROBLEM THIS TIME...

PRISM OF
PARTISAN PRIAPISM

CO-BRANDING SOLUTIONS FOR MODERN POLITICS

BY LLOYD DANGLE

DEMS! REPS!

FAT ASS ®

ONE PARTY WITHOUT THE PARTISANSHIP... **HELLO FAT ASS!**

The **ethanoil** ® PARTY!

WE'RE **FOND** OF **FUEL!**

THE **Abortion** maybe? ™ PARTY

STAYING **FLUID** ON THE **FETUS**

Skybox Suite

POLITICAL PARTY & CLUB ®

WHERE THE CUSTOMER ALWAYS COMES FIRST!

THE **NU-KINDA** ® PARTY!

WHERE THE NEW KIND OF DEMOCRATS **MERGE** WITH THE NEW KIND OF REPUBLICANS!

NU-KINDA? U-BETCHA!

THE **ABE ROOSEVELT** PARTY ®

MORPHING THE PARTIES OF LINCOLN AND FDR— AND ABANDONING ALL THEIR PRINCIPLES!

HEY, SWEATY! ®

HA! HA!

THE PARTY WHERE THE JOKE IS **ALWAYS** ON THE UNION GUY!

☆ PROFESSIONAL ☆ **POLLWATCHERS** PARTY ☆ ®

? ?

I LIKE GUM. 52% YES 48% NO

CRACKER

SERVING UP MIDDLE-OF-THE-ROAD SOUTHERN-STYLE CANDIDATES FOR YEARS!

VOTE **CRACKER,** EMINENTLY ELECTABLE.

TROUBLETOWN

A VICE PRESIDENTIAL CANDIDATE WHO IS A **JEW**! THIS IS NEWS!

WE'RE SO PROUD OF IT.

DOES THIS MEAN MATZO BALL SOUP WILL ALWAYS BE ON THE MENU AT THE WHITE HOUSE?

DO YOU ALWAYS WEAR A **YARMULKE**— EVEN IN THE SHOWER?

HA! HA!

ARE **ALL** JEWS FOR VOUCHER SCHOOLS?

IN A CRISIS, WOULD YOU FIRST CONSULT WITH THE OLD TESTAMENT OR THE WALL STREET JOURNAL?

WHAT IS A "MENSCH?"

ARE JEWS COMPLETELY INCAPACITATED DURING RELIGIOUS HOLIDAYS?

AREN'T YOU AFRAID OF ALIENATING THE VOTERS WHO IDENTIFY THEMSELVES AS RABID, ANTI-SEMITIC BIGOTS?

NOT IN THE LEAST...

BECAUSE OUR FUTURE COMMERCE SECRETARY WILL BE DISCREDITED HOLOCAUST REVISIONIST, ANTHONY FLEGGI!

I'VE BEEN KICKED OUT OF EVERY MAJOR UNIVERSITY FOR MY VIEWS.

SEE, AL GORE ISN'T AFRAID TO EMBRACE THOSE WITH DIFFERENT— EVEN REPULSIVE— VIEWS. THAT'S WHAT OUR PARTY IS ALL ABOUT!

YOU'RE A WUSS, PAT BUCHANAN!

TROUBLETOWN

BY LLOYD DANGLE

THE REPUBLICANS WILL DROP 200,000 BALLOONS AT THIS CONVENTION, WHICH IS 5% MORE THAN THE DEMOCRATS AND 100% MORE THAN RALPH NADER!

OH GOD! WHY DID YOU EVEN MENTION **NADER**, ELAINE?!

G.O.P FESTIVAL OF FREEDOM

NOTHING SEEMS TO MAKE CAMPAIGN COVERAGE GO FROM VAPID TO VENOMOUS LIKE THE INTRODUCTION OF RALPH NADER!

I'D LIKE TO KNOW WHAT THE **HELL** HE THINKS HE'S DOING!

WHETHER HE KNOWS HIMSELF IS THE QUESTION.

G.O.P. FESTIVAL OF FREEDOM

OF COURSE NOW THERE ARE A LOT OF STORIES COMING OUT OF WASHINGTON THAT SUGGEST HE'S NOT AS "**DECENT**" AS PORTRAYED, ALTHOUGH I CAN'T GO INTO DETAIL ON THOSE RUMORS.

THAT'S DISTURBING.

IT CERTAINLY IS. AND, YOU KNOW, NADER **OWNS STOCK** AND IS ACTUALLY A **MILLIONAIRE** FROM FLEECING IDEALISTIC COLLEGE STUDENTS!

I ASSUMED HE SLEPT IN A FLOP HOUSE! WHAT ELSE DON'T WE KNOW?

AND WHY SHOULD HE BE ALLOWED TO **STEAL** VOTES FROM THE REAL CANDIDATES WHO'VE BEEN SUCKING UP TO DONORS FOR DECADES?!

IT'S THE PRICE WE PAY FOR DEMOCRACY.

POOR GORE!

OH MY, THE TELEVISION INFOMERCIAL ON GEORGE W. BUSH'S LIFE IS STARTING...

THE GOP OUTSPENT DEMOCRATS BY 35% ON INFOMERCIALS! I'VE HEARD THIS MOVIE IS AS GOOD AS "THE GREEN MILE."

troubletown

BY LLOYD DANGLE

THE COMBINATION OF BENADRYL AND THE PRESIDENTIAL RACE HAVE PITCHED ME INTO A DEEP, SUMMER LETHARGY.

SO DEEP IN FACT, I ALMOST FORGOT THAT POLITIXYUKS4U.COM WAS SENDING ME TO THE REPUBLICAN NATIONAL CONVENTION, AND PAYING ME A HEFTY FEE TO REPORT BY STREAMING LIVE FEED!

GOING MY WAY?

ON AMTRACK, I'M SEATED NEXT TO DR. LAURA SCHLESSINGER!

THE CONVENTION IS BEING HELD IN A MEXICAN RESTAURANT WITH A HOT TUB. DR. LAURA INTRODUCES ME TO GARY BAUER AND CHARLTON HESTON.

WHO WANTS TO PARTY?

NOT NOW, DR. LAURA. YOUR FRIEND MUST HELP US WITH OUR ABORTION PLANK.

G.W. HIMSELF IS ABOUT TO GIVE A TOAST WHEN RALPH NADER DRIVES INTO THE RESTAURANT IN A GRAY CORVAIR.

I'M PROUD OF MY HISPANIC HERITAGE!

THE TACOS HERE ARE UNSAFE AT ANY SPEED.

GORE APPEARS IN A SCOUT UNIFORM AND LUNGES TOWARD MR. NADER WITH A PITCHER OF SANGRIA!

WATCH OUT, RALPH!

WHY, YOU...

DUCK!

SWOOSH!

SNAP OUT OF IT, UNCLE! YOU'RE SUPPOSED TO TAKE ME TO CHICKEN RUN!!

IT'S THE BENADRYL. TELL AUNTIE SHE'D BETTER DRIVE.

TROUBLE TOWN

BY LLOYD DANGLE

Panel 1: DAD, IF THE POLLS AIN'T WRONG YOUR LEAST INTELLECTUALLY CURIOUS OR AMBITIOUS SON IS ABOUT TO BECOME PRESIDENT! — THAT'S MY BOY!

Panel 2: CHENEY, JAMES BAKER III, PACK YOUR STIFF WHITE SHIRTS! OUR PEOPLE ARE BACK IN STYLE! — YES SIR, MR. PRESIDENT... — TEAM BUSH

Panel 3: DID WE GET THE WHITE HOUSE BACK, DAD? — YES, JEB. WE SENT THOSE HILLBILLIES PACKING! — CALL YOUR PREP SCHOOL FRIENDS WHO NEED JOBS.

Panel 4: NOW WAIT A DOGGONE MINUTE. AH'M NOT OF WARSHINGTON! I'M A SLANGY, TWANGY, DIFF'RNT KIND OF BUSH. — I GOTTA DO THINGS MY OWN WAY.

Panel 5: YOU LIKED IT WHEN YOU NEEDED OIL WELLS AND BASEBALL TEAMS, BUT NOW YOU'RE TOO **GOOD** FOR US **BLUEBLOODS?** DON'T CALL ME WHEN THE DOO-DOO STARTS RISING! — NO! — I TAKE IT ALL BACK!

Panel 6: I'D **LOVE** TO SERVE IN ANOTHER BUSH ADMINISTRATION! YOUR DAD ALWAYS SAID I REMINDED HIM OF YOU! — OFFICE OF DAN QUA...

TROUBLETOWN

BY LLOYD DANGLE

INAUGURATION DAY ARRIVES AND THERE'S STILL NO WINNER! FOR THE SAKE OF THE NATION, BUSH AND GORE AGREE TO CO-CHAIR THE PRESIDENCY!

WE SOLEMNLY SWEAR...

I SOLUM-NEMLY...

HEY! ME FIRST!

THE BUSH FORCES TAKE THE EAST WING OF THE WHITE HOUSE, THE GORE CAMP TAKES THE WEST WING—AND A DISPUTE ARISES!

THIS IS JAMES BAKER. WE HAVEN'T RECEIVED ACCESS TO ANY TOWELS!

WE DEMAND AN IMMEDIATE COUNT OF THE HAND TOWELS!

WARREN CHRISTOPHER GOES ON THE OFFENSIVE, FOCUSING HIS ATTENTION ON "CHAFFED SCRIMLETS."

THOSE ARE THE LITTLE CRUMBS THAT FALL INTO THE BOTTOM OF THE TOASTER!

THE CLASHES INTENSIFY:

THIS INJUNCTION TO STOP THE GORES' EXCESSIVELY NOISY LOVEMAKING IS PURELY A CASE OF SOUR GRAPES!

BUSH MOVES TO REINSTATE HIS DAD AND THE ENTIRE '88 TEAM.

IT'S YOUR FAULT I DIDN'T WIN! NOW YOU TAKE OVER!

NO PROB, JUNIOR.

HOW THE BUSHGORE PRESIDENTS WILL LEAD REMAINS TO BE SEEN. FIRST JUSTICE CLARENCE THOMAS WILL HAVE TO CAST THE DECIDING VOTE ON WHO GETS FIRST BATHROOM PRIVILEGES.

GIMME!

NO! STOP IT!

?

LET GO!

OW!

TROUBLETOWN

THE CURRENT FUROR OVER **CHADS**, BOTH DIMPLED AND PREGNANT, ONCE AGAIN ILLUSTRATES AMERICANS' ABYSMAL IGNORANCE OF HISTORY.

CHADS HAVE PLAYED A CRUCIAL ROLE.

ALEXANDER HAMILTON WAS KILLED WHEN HIS REVOLVER JAMMED ON A **CRUMPLED CHAD.**

BLASTED CHAD!

POP!

IN THE 1960 KENNEDY-NIXON DEBATE, THE WASHINGTON POST DESCRIBED NIXON'S SWEAT AS **DRIBBLING CHADS.**

THOSE STREAMING CHADS COST HIM.

PRESIDENT McKINLEY DIED CHOKING ON A SMALL, SEED-LIKE **CHAD.**

LODGED IN HIS WINDPIPE FOR A CENTURY!

GEORGE WASHINGTON'S TROOPS MUTINIED TWICE BECAUSE THEY WERE SICK OF BEING PAID IN **REVOLUTIONARY CHADS.**

EITHER THAT OR WIG POWDER.

THE TITANIC CRASHED INTO AN ICEBURG WHILE STEERING TO AVOID AN ICY, **ATLANTIC CHAD.**

CHAD AHOY!

WHEN NIKITA KRUSHCHEV TOOK OFF HIS SHOE AT THE UNITED NATIONS HE WAS REALLY TRYING TO REMOVE A **PAINFUL CHAD!**

HOW DARE ME!

I VILL BURY THIS CHAD!

ABRAHAM LINCOLN CARRIED A HANDFUL OF **CHADS** IN HIS HAT!

THEY WERE DOUSED WITH VINEGAR.

THE NAME OF RONALD REAGAN'S HAIR STYLIST WAS **CHAD.**

YOU'RE A GENIUS, CHAD.

TROUBLETOWN

BY LLOYD DANGLE

BIG NEWS: CLINTON STOLE WHITE HOUSE SILVERWARE AND PARDONED A BILLIONAIRE SLEAZEBALL BENEFACTOR FOR PAYBACK!

HERE'S YOUR PARDON, KIND SIR.

OH, MY.

PARDON

WHITE HOUSE

AT THE CONSORTIUM OF CLINTON-HATERS, A CONSERVATIVE THINK TANK WITH A $500 MILLION/YR. ENDOWMENT, THIS CAME AS WELCOME NEWS.

NOT AGAIN!

THIS TIME WE'VE GOT HIM FOR SURE!

IT'S TOO BAD THAT WE FAILED TO RUIN HIS PRESIDENCY, BUT WE'LL TAKE WHAT WE CAN GET!

HE'LL SLITHER OUT OF IT AND MAKE FOOLS OF US.

NOW WE MUST TAINT THE LEGACY! IT WILL BE SWEET CONSOLATION IF BILL CLINTON IS ALWAYS REMEMBERED FOR THESE FINAL ACTS!

INSTEAD OF BONKING MONICA?

THIS IS NO GENNIFER FLOWERS! IT'S STEALING AND CURRYING FAVOR TO THE RICH! PEOPLE WON'T FORGIVE THAT!

MEANWHILE, GEORGE W. BUSH STEALS THE ELECTION AND GIVES HIS BILLIONAIRE SLEAZE-BALL BENEFACTORS A $TRILLION TAX BREAK!

COMPASSIONATE!

BOING!

BOING!

THE WIND IS OUTTA HERE

A DANGEROUSLY CLOSE PARODY

THE SCENE IS A SOUTHERN PLANTATION ON THE BANKS OF THE POTOMAC:

OH DADDY, I LOVE IT HERE. REPUBLICANS WILL ALWAYS RULE THE SENATE WON'T WE?

THAT'S RIGHT JEFFORDS, HONEY.

JEFFORDS DEAR, I WANT YOU TO MARRY GROVER NORQUIST.

BUT HE'S A RED MEAT REPUBLICAN! HE'S NOT MY TYPE!

WHO CARES?

YOU'LL MARRY A RED MEAT REPUBLICAN IF I SAY SO! I'M MAJORITY LEADER AROUND HERE!

SMACK!

JUST THEN, A DASHING STRANGER, RHETT DASCHLE, APPROACHES...

FRANKLY, MY DEAR, I DON'T GIVE A DAMN.

JEFFORDS, COME BACK! THE SENATE WILL NEVER BE THE SAME!

CLOP!

CLOP!

YOO HOO! WHAT ABOUT US SOUTHERN DEMOCRAT DEBUTANTS?

WE'RE NOT SPOKEN FOR.

TROUBLETOWN

BY LLOYD DANGLE

KAREN HUGHS AND KARL ROVE STRATEGIZE FOR THE PRESIDENT.

WHAT THE HELL ARE WE GOING TO DO?

WELL, AT LEAST THE ECONOMY CAN'T GET ANY WORSE.

HOWDY! I FEEL REFRESHED! LET'S GET TO WORK AND SPEND THAT SURPLUS!

UH, DUBYA, THERE'S SOME BAD NEWS...

THE SURPLUS IS GONE.

HAW! HAW! HAW! C'MON, THAT'S FUZZY MATH!

HA! HA! HA!

NO, REALLY. THERE'S NO MONEY.

PROCEED NOW WITH THE THE SPACE SHIELD!

WE'LL HAVE TO DIP INTO SOCIAL SECURITY,

THE $300 REBATE WILL JUMP START THE ECONOMY!

AMERICANS HAVE ALREADY BLOWN THAT MONEY ON BOOZE, GASOLINE & LOTTO TICKETS!

BUY ALL NEW MILITARY EQUIPMENT!

EVERY SCHOOL IN AMERICA MUST HAVE A SHINY, NEW GYMNASIUM FLOOR!

THAT WILL BANKRUPT MEDICARE!

KARL, KAREN, READ MY LIPS... **NO NEW TAXES!!**

NOT THOSE WORDS!

GOD, NO!

IT'S POSSIBLE THAT HE'S GENETICALLY PROGRAMMED TO BE A ONE-TERM PRESIDENT.

43

TROUBLETOWN

BY LLOYD DANGLE

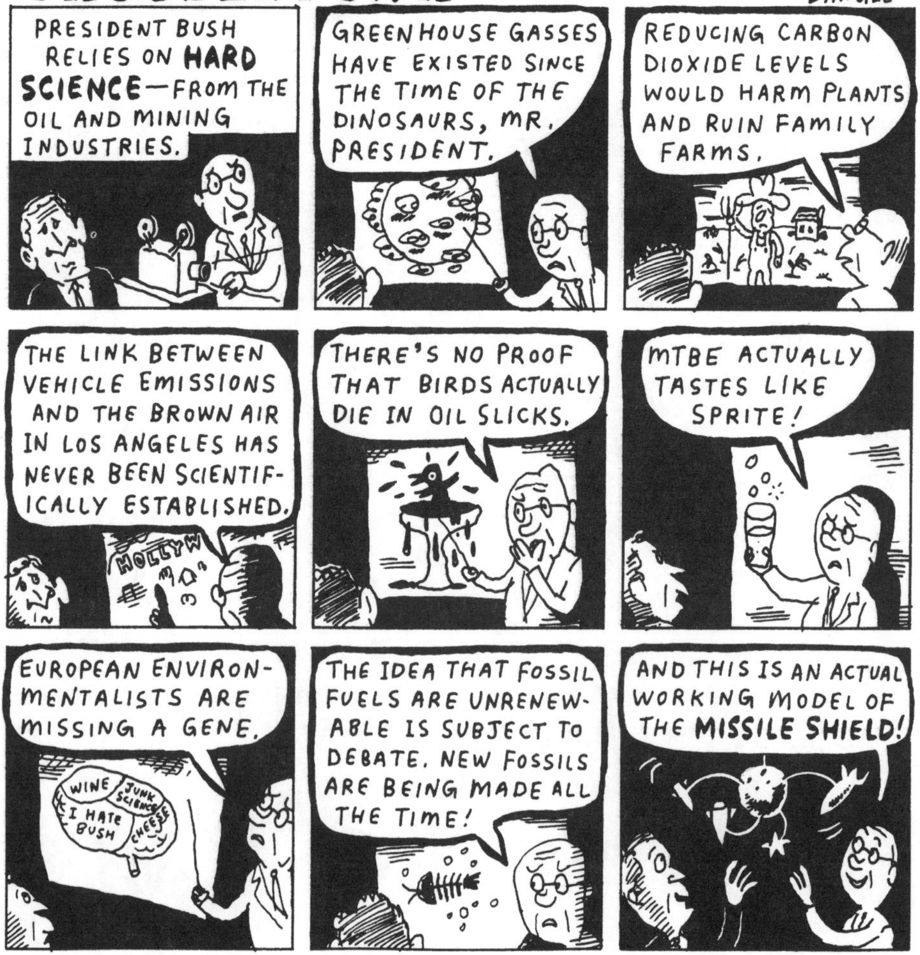
PRESIDENT BUSH RELIES ON **HARD SCIENCE**—FROM THE OIL AND MINING INDUSTRIES.
GREENHOUSE GASSES HAVE EXISTED SINCE THE TIME OF THE DINOSAURS, MR. PRESIDENT.
REDUCING CARBON DIOXIDE LEVELS WOULD HARM PLANTS AND RUIN FAMILY FARMS.
THE LINK BETWEEN VEHICLE EMISSIONS AND THE BROWN AIR IN LOS ANGELES HAS NEVER BEEN SCIENTIFICALLY ESTABLISHED.
HOLLYW
THERE'S NO PROOF THAT BIRDS ACTUALLY DIE IN OIL SLICKS.
MTBE ACTUALLY TASTES LIKE SPRITE!
EUROPEAN ENVIRONMENTALISTS ARE MISSING A GENE.
WINE
JUNK SCIENCE
I HATE BUSH
CHEESE
THE IDEA THAT FOSSIL FUELS ARE UNRENEWABLE IS SUBJECT TO DEBATE. NEW FOSSILS ARE BEING MADE ALL THE TIME!
AND THIS IS AN ACTUAL WORKING MODEL OF THE **MISSILE SHIELD**!

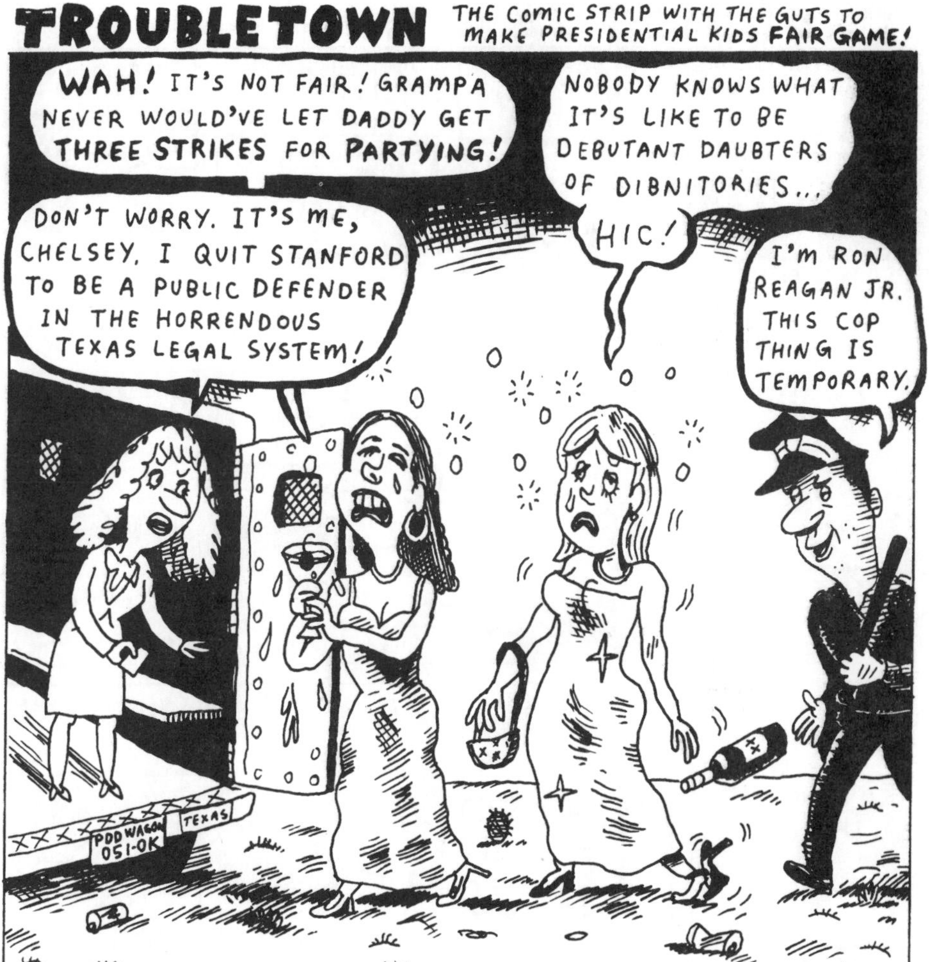
TROUBLETOWN
THE COMIC STRIP WITH THE GUTS TO MAKE PRESIDENTIAL KIDS FAIR GAME!
WAH! IT'S NOT FAIR! GRAMPA NEVER WOULD'VE LET DADDY GET THREE STRIKES FOR PARTYING!
NOBODY KNOWS WHAT IT'S LIKE TO BE DEBUTANT DAUBTERS OF DIBNITORIES...
HIC!
DON'T WORRY. IT'S ME, CHELSEY. I QUIT STANFORD TO BE A PUBLIC DEFENDER IN THE HORRENDOUS TEXAS LEGAL SYSTEM!
I'M RON REAGAN JR. THIS COP THING IS TEMPORARY.
POD WAGON 051-OK
TEXAS

TROUBLETOWN

BY LLOYD DANGLE

SECRETARY OF THE DEPARTMENT OF FISH & WILDLIFE

SAM STENKY, PRESIDENT & CEO, STENKY CYANIDE

PEDOPHILIA PREVENTION CZAR

BISHOP FLANNGHAN McELROY

OVERSEER OF ELECTIONS: LYNN APPLEBEE

CEO OF APPLEBEE BALLOT SHREDDERS

SUPREME COURT JUSTICE

KA-CHING!

HUGH DIBBLE, NO. 5 ALL-TIME "PIONEER CLUB" FUNDRAISER

NATIONAL LABOR RELATIONS BOARD

THE STAFF OF WE BUST'EM UNION EXTERMINATORS

JOINT CHIEFS

WHO US? NO, WE ONLY LOOK LIKE FORMER ENRON EXECUTIVES! NYCK! NYCK!

UNDERSECRETARY TO U.N. AMBASSADOR NEGROPONTE

"GUS" PINOCHET

CHAIRMAN OF THE UNITED FOOD SAFETY COUNCIL

EDWARD COLI

HEAD OF THE S.E.C.

I ONLY RESEMBLE A FORMER ENRON CEO!

JOHN DOE

SECRETARIES OF THE ARMY, NAVY, AIR FORCE, AND MARINES.

OUR BEST EVER!

THE SALES STAFF OF GENERAL DYNAMICS.

9TH DISTRICT FEDERAL COURT JUDGE

SHOW ME DA MONEY!

RAY PIDDLETON, NO. 9 "PIONEER" FUNDRAISER

CHIEF MIDEAST PEACE NEGOTIATOR

STU HOOPER, CEO OF ACCU-BLAST INC., MAKERS OF STRAP-ON DYNAMITE BELTS

TROUBLETOWN

CONSPIRATOR COMEBACKS

BY LLOYD DANGLE

CONVICTED IRAN-CONTRA CONSPIRATOR JOHN POINDEXTER WILL HEAD THE NEW INFORMATION AWARENESS OFFICE.

YOU WANT THE CONSTITUTION SUBVERTED? I'M YOUR MAN!

OLLIE NORTH WILL BE NATIONAL SECURITY ADVISOR TO THE "SHADOW GOVERNMENT."

AS LONG AS I CAN STILL BE A SHOCK JOCK.

DRUG-RUNNER FELIX "CHI CHI" RODRIGUEZ WILL HEAD UP THE FEDERAL AVIATION SAFETY ADMINISTRATION.

I KNOW HOW TO FLY WITH IT REALLY LOADED DOWN.

THE WATERGATE "PLUMBERS" WILL BE FEDERAL CIRCUIT COURT JUDGES.

HEAR YE! ALL RISE FOR THE HONORABLE BURGLARS.

SPIRO AGNEW'S FROZEN BRAIN WILL HEAD UP THE OFFICE OF CAMPAIGN REFORM

SHRED THE DOCUMENTS? YES, SIR.

JOHN NEGROPONTE AND ELLIOT ABRAHMS FORM A SECRET USO COMEDY DUO, TO ENTERTAIN LATIN AMERICAN DEATH SQUADS.

WHO'S BEEN TORTURED.

NO! WHO HAS BEEN DISAPPEARED!

"LATE" CIA DIRECTOR WILLIAM CASEY WILL HEAD THE SECRET "SHADOW POLICE."

PREPARE TO PROVIDE DENIABILITY!

GEORGE BUSH I, HR HALDEMAN, FAWN HALL, KENNETH LAY, AND FRANK CARLUCCI FORM THE SECRET FOSSIL FUEL TAX BREAK COMMISSION.

OUR DECISIONS ARE BINDING—EVEN THOUGH THIS MEETING NEVER HAPPENED.

NANCY REAGAN WILL OPERATE THE OFFICE OF ASTROLOGICAL PROJECTION AND CEANCE AFFAIRS.

GOOD NEWS! LEE ATWATER IS AVAILABLE FOR SOME DIRTY TRICKS.

TROUBLETOWN

JUNIOR'S QUID PRO QUO

BY LLOYD DANGLE

FREE SUPREME COURT SKYBOX AT RANGERS GAMES.

CHENEY WILL TAKE CARE OF THEIR DRY CLEANING FOR AS LONG AS JUNIOR IS IN OFFICE.

DOLLAR CLEANERS

FREE SPICE CHANNEL FOR CLARENCE THOMAS.

THAT'S WHAT I'M TALKING ABOUT.

JEB PASSES FLORIDA LAW OUTLAWING COVER CHARGES FOR SUPREME COURT JUSTICES AT WET T-SHIRT CONTESTS.

DUKE

CHRISTINE WHITMAN WILL TAKE JUSTICE SCALIA ALONG WHEN SHE GOES "PROFILING" WITH JERSEY TROOPERS.

HA HA! HA HA

ADOLF COORS WILL UNDERWRITE SWEARING-IN CEREMONIES.

POP A COLD ONE FOR THE UNBORN.

ANY TIME A SUPREME COURT JUSTICE WANTS TO PARTY, POPPY & BAR WILL CLEAR OUT OF KENNEBUNKPORT.

BUSH SR.

THE REPUBLICAN JUSTICES WILL GET SPECIAL ATTENTION AT NEWT GINGRICH SEMINARS.

THE SEATS IN FRONT ARE RESERVED.

CHIEF JUSTICE REHNQUIST GETS A DORMITORY NAMED AFTER HIM AT BOB JONES UNIVERSITY.

JOHN ASHCROFT

TROUBLETOWN

EVER SINCE HE GOT TOUGH ON OSAMA, PRESIDENT BUSH IS UNTOUCHABLE!

ANYBODY WHO SAYS HE'S A NITWIT OR A DUMMY IS GUILTY OF TREASON!

PREPARE YE TO DIE!

QUESTION THE SECRET MILITARY TRIBUNALS AND YOU'RE A TALIBAN-LOVING ENABLER OF EVIL!

MAKE FUN OF HIS INARTICULATE SPEECH, YOU GET LAMBASTED BY DINNER GUESTS!

I OUGHTA THROW THESE MASHED POTATOES IN YOUR FACE!

JOURNALISTS KNOW HE CAN HAVE ALL THE AFFAIRS WITH INTERNS HE WANTS; THEY BETTER KEEP IT ZIPPED!

REPORT ON HIS DAUGHTERS' DRINKING AND YOU IMMEDIATELY GET DROPPED BY EIGHTEEN NEWSPAPERS.

I SHOULD'VE SELF CENSORED.

BUSH BABES WASTED

FIRED!

TALK ABOUT HOW MUCH TIME HE SPENDS ON THE RANCH VACATIONING, AND FIREMEN WILL COME AND KICK YOUR ASS.

CRITICIZE THE PLAN TO CUT TAXES WHILE SPENDING $20 BILLION MORE ON MILITARY; YOUR MOTHER VOWS NEVER TO SPEAK TO YOU AGAIN!

LAST WILL & TESTAMENT

MAKE HIM LOOK FUNNY, AND YOU GET HAULED BEFORE THE CARICA-TURISTS LEAGUE.

YOU ARE DIS-QUILLED!

SNATCH!

TROUBLETOWN

BY LLOYD DANGLE

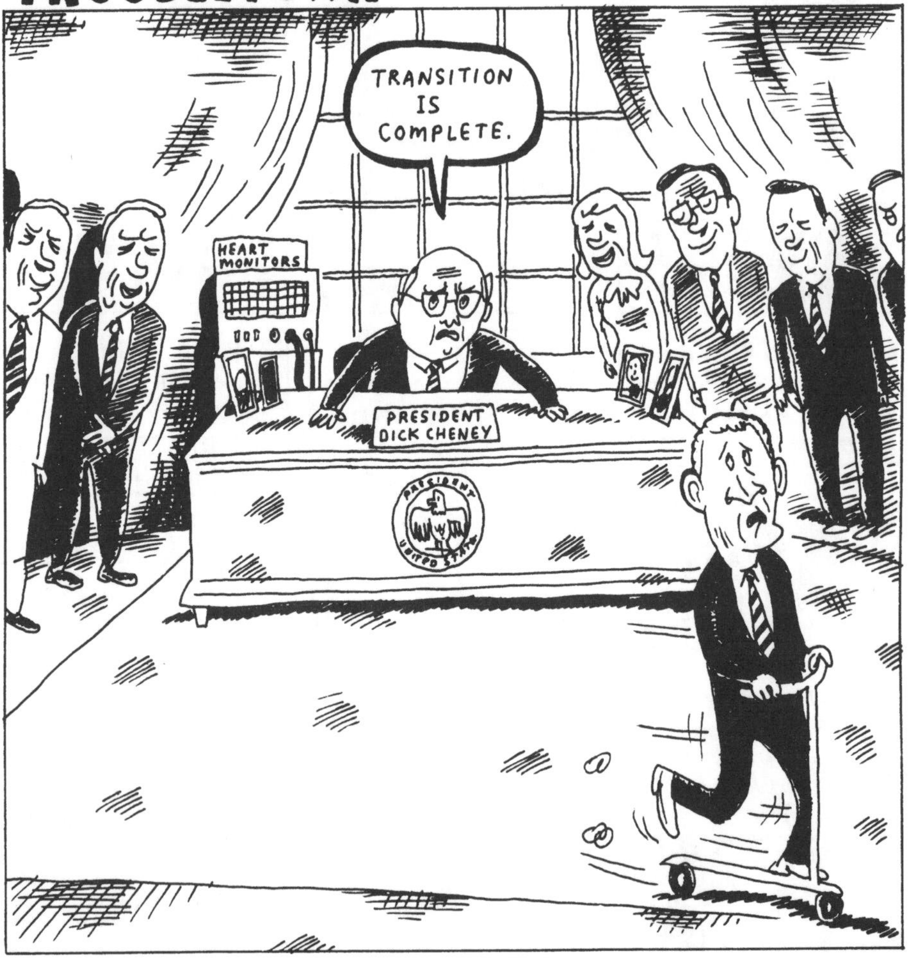
TRANSITION IS COMPLETE.
HEART MONITORS
PRESIDENT DICK CHENEY

TROUBLETOWN

BY LLOYD DANGLE

AFTER VANQUISHING THE DEMOCRATIC HORDES, EMPEROR BUSHIVUS II DEPOSED HIS CHIEF RIVAL IN THE SENATE.

FEED HIM TO THE MEDIA!

AW, C'MON NOW!

AND SO, BUSHIVUS II AND HIS CONSULS RULED THE EMPIRE!

SIGH! MY ARMIES ARE INVINCIBLE, YET I WORRY THEY STILL TOO SMALL.

HAIL BUSHIVUS!

HE WAS ADVISED BY HIS MOST LOYAL CONSUL, DICKUS CHENEYCUS.

YOU, BUSHIVUS, MUST CONTROL ALL THE ENERGY THAT COMES FROM THE SUN!

MEANWHILE, BUSHIVUS'S PREOCCUPATION WITH CONQUERING THE BARBARIANS ALLOWED STRAINS TO DEVELOP AT HOME.

I CAN'T EVEN AFFORD A STATE COLLEGE!

MY PRESCRIPTION RAN OUT, DEAR SCHOLAR.

I WILL DIE.

AND THE OBSCENE WEALTH OF THE OVERCLASS LED TO AN ORGY OF EXCESS, CORPULENCE AND DEPRAVITY.

HEY, CHECK IT OUT LADIES, VIAGRA!

CEOS ONLY

AND SO, INEVITABLY, HUBRIS LED TO THE EMPIRE'S DECLINE AND BUSHIVUS II WAS SACKED.

HARK! THE GREAT BABY-BOOMER RETIREE WAR IS OVER! VICTORY IS OURS!

AARP

RHOMBUS OF
THE RIDICULOUS

TROUBLETOWN

BY LLOYD DANGLE

SO, HOW ARE YOU FEELING? IS THE ZOLOFT-PAXIL-WELLBUTRIN MEDLEY HELPING YOUR DEPRESSION?

YEAH, I FEEL JUST LIKE TONY SOPRANO.

I LOVE THAT SHOW.

THE INSURANCE WOULDN'T COVER IT, THOUGH, SO IT COST $196! IS THERE AN ALTERNATIVE?

???

AHHHH!! ☆#₮✆!! DAMN!

WHENEVER I PRESCRIBE SOMETHING THAT ACTUALLY WORKS, THE INSURANCE COMPANY SCREWS IT UP!

LEMME TELL YA, IF YOU THINK THIS ENERGY CRISIS IS BAD? WELL IT'S **NOTHING** COMPARED TO HEALTH CARE CRISIS THAT'S COMING! IT'S COMING!

THINGS WILL GET WORSE!

OKAY, LET'S SEE WHAT THOSE MAGGOTS WILL ALLOW ME TO PRESCRIBE FOR YOU.

AH, TO HELL WITH IT! HERE'S FIVE YEAR'S WORTH OF FREE SAMPLES. WHO KNOWS IF YOU'LL EVER BE BACK!

TROUBLETOWN

ARTICLE 1: INSURANCE COMPANIES MUST GIVE A REASON FOR DENYING YOU COVERAGE.

WE DON'T COVER KIDNEY OPERATIONS BECAUSE THEY BEGIN WITH THE LETTER "K."

ARTICLE 2: MAGAZINES DATING BACK FOR MORE THAN SEVEN YEARS MUST BE REMOVED FROM DOCTORS' WAITING ROOMS.

THIS WAS A NEW ISSUE WHEN I GOT HERE.

LIFE — AT HOME WITH J.F.K.

ARTICLE 3: THE 44 MILLION UNINSURED ARE ENTITLED TO A SELF-CARE BROCHURE, ANNUALLY.

EASY BREAST SELF EXAM — TRY IT!

ARTICLE 4: PATIENTS ARE ENTITLED TO ONE FREE BIOPSY EVERY TIME THEIR PREMIUMS ARE JACKED UP BY 50% OR MORE.

MY THIRD THIS YEAR!

ARTICLE 5: VIAGRA AND OTHER ESSENTIAL DRUGS FOR OLD, WHITE CONGRESSMEN MUST BE 100% COVERED.

100% BALDNESS
100% PENIS ACTIVATION
PLAN II
100% PROSTATE
FULL HIP REPLACEMENT

ARTICLE 6: ELDERLY AND OTHER "PROFIT-NEGATIVE" PATIENTS RECEIVE FREE LIP SERVICE EVERY FOUR YEARS.

FREE Rx REFILL WHEN YOU FILL OUT YOUR ABSENTEE BALLOT!

ARTICLE 7: AFTER 17 EMERGENCY ROOM VISITS, UNINSURED CHILDREN IN TEXAS WIN A FREE BACON CHEESEBURGER.

LET ME STAMP YOUR "SICK REWARDS" CARD, HONEY!

ARTICLE 8: PATIENTS MUST GIVE CONSENT BEFORE DOCTORS CAN SEND TINY CAMERAS TO EXPLORE THEIR BODY CAVITIES FOR TV.

HA! HA!

HERE COMES THE URETHRA. CHOO! CHOO!

INSURANCE COMPANY WELL-BEING GUARANTEE:

THIS ISN'T ONE OF THOSE HILLARY THINGS.

TAKE A BIG TAX CUT AND CALL ME IN THE MORNING.

DON'T WORRY.

TROUBLETOWN

BY LLOYD DANGLE

I DID IT, DAVE! I FINISHED COUNTING THE GENES IN THE HUMAN GENOME! IT'S **30,000**!

WHAT'S THE MATTER, DAVE? AREN'T YOU EXCITED?

TO BE HONEST I'M DISAPPOINTED. A JELLYFISH HAS 27,000 GENES!

A PIECE OF STRING CHEESE HAS 20,000! WHAT KIND OF NUMBER IS 30K?!! IT'S LESS THAN THE GENES IN RICE!

SIZE DOESN'T MATTER!

KEEP TELLING YOURSELF THAT, BILL! HOW MANY HIGHLY EVOLVED BEINGS CAN HAVE THEIR ENTIRE ESSENCE DOWNLOADED ONTO A FLOPPY IN 3 MINUTES?!

HOLD ON THERE! GOD'S CHILDREN DID **NOT** EVOLVE FROM BACTERIA!

ATTORNEY GENERAL ASHCROFT?

UNDER MY NEW FAITH-BASED LAW ENFORCEMENT, I'M IMPOSING A GAG RULE ON THIS DISCOVERY!

FOR GOD'S SAKE, ANNOINT ME! I NEED TO BELIEVE!

TROUBLETOWN

BY LLOYD DANGLE

Panel 1:
WHAT AM I LOOKING AT HERE?

THOSE ARE HUMAN **STEM CELLS** FROM A DISCARDED SIX-CELL EMBRYO, SENATOR.

Panel 2:
SO THOSE ARE THE LITTLE BASTARDS WHO ARE CREATING IDEOLOGICAL PROBLEMS FOR ME?!

YES, SIR.

Panel 3:
THEY EVEN LOOK LIKE STEMS!

THAT'S WHAT THE DEVIL WANTS YOU TO BELIEVE, SENATOR.

Panel 4:
THOSE STEMS COULD GROW UP TO BE FLAXEN-HAIRED CHILDREN!

STEMS LIKE THOSE COULD CURE CANCER, PARKINSONS, AND ERECTILE DYSFUNCTION!

Panel 5:
I MUST RUN THIS ISSUE THROUGH A GEOGRAPHICAL RELIGIO-POLITIK LITMUS TEST!

DON'T FORGET THE CHRISTIAN COALITION!

DON'T FORGET PHARMACEUTICAL COMPANIES!

Panel 6:
WELL? WHICH WAY DO YOU THINK HE'LL JUMP?

WHAT DO I LOOK LIKE — A DIVINING ROD?!!

TROUBLETOWN

SENATOR BUMFORD IS FLUMMOXED.

SHOULD I JOIN MY REPUBLICAN COLLEAGUES, THE POPE, AND MANY EVANGELISTS IN OPPOSING EMBRYO STEM CELL RESEARCH?

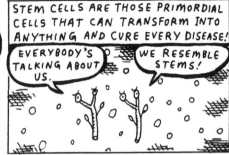

STEM CELLS ARE THOSE PRIMORDIAL CELLS THAT CAN TRANSFORM INTO ANYTHING AND CURE EVERY DISEASE!

EVERYBODY'S TALKING ABOUT US.

WE RESEMBLE STEMS!

AND, THEY COME FROM HYPER-STIMULATED, INFERTILE COUPLES!

GOOD NEWS! **THIRTY** HEALTHY EMBRYOS! WANNA TRY FOR THIRTYUPLETS?

EIGHT IS MY MAX.

LAB

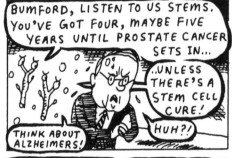

BUMFORD, LISTEN TO US STEMS. YOU'VE GOT FOUR, MAYBE FIVE YEARS UNTIL PROSTATE CANCER SETS IN...

..UNLESS THERE'S A STEM CELL CURE!

HUH?!

THINK ABOUT ALZHEIMERS!

STEM CELLS CAN'T TALK! THAT'S ONE OF SATAN'S TRICKS! DON'T FORGET WHO GOT YOU ELECTED!

EVANGELICAL CHRISTIANS!

BLOCK THE EMBRYO KILLING AND WE'LL KEEP YOU IN OFFICE FOR ANOTHER 20 YEARS!

SUPPORT STEMS AND WE'LL KEEP STROM THURMOND ALIVE FOR ANOTHER 100 YEARS!

TROUBLETOWN

BY LLOYD DANGLE

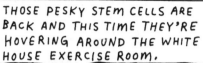

THOSE PESKY STEM CELLS ARE BACK AND THIS TIME THEY'RE HOVERING AROUND THE WHITE HOUSE EXERCISE ROOM.

WE CAN CURE ANYTHING!

WE CAN HELP GROW MUSCLE TISSUE!

WE CAN HELP TO FIX YOUR SYNTAX!

DYSLEXIA MAY BE CURABLE THROUGH RESEARCH!

HELP! DICK! I'M BEING PURSUED BY TWIGS!

OFFICE OF DICK CHENEY

WE CAN MAKE A MISSILE DEFENSE SHIELD THAT WORKS!

GET IN HERE! HELP ME STUFF SOME TOWELS UNDER THE DOOR!

YANK!

LAST WEEK THEY CORNERED ME AND SAID THEY COULD DEVELOP A HEALTHY KIND OF PASTRAMI.

MAYBE FEDERAL DOLLARS WOULD MAKE THEM GO AWAY!

KNOCK! KNOCK!

I DOUBT IT.

DICK REMINDS THE PRESIDENT WHAT THE POPE SAID: RIVERS OF FIRE WILL FLOW FROM MOUNT ETNA UNTIL THE STEMS ARE PURGED!

MEANWHILE, IN THE LAB:

WE'VE DONE IT! WE'VE CREATED THE ULTIMATE LOBBYIST!

WHAT IF HE FELL INTO THE WRONG HANDS?

ACE

ACE CO.

ACE DRUG MFG.

TROUBLETOWN

REPORT FROM NATURE

BY LLOYD DANGLE

OUT IN YELLOWSTONE THE WOLVES AND GRIZZLIES ARE MAKING A COMEBACK!

GRRR!

BUT THEIR AVERSION TO CROWDS HAS LET BISON, ELK, MARMOTS, DEER, CARIBOU AND ANTELOPE PROLIFERATE ABUNDANTLY.

I ALMOST BACKED OVER A MOOSE IN THE SKI LODGE PARKING LOT!

MOVE IT OR PARK IT, BULLWINKLE!

TRASH

GUESTS ONLY

INDEED MOTHER NATURE DEPENDS ON THE RV, THE SUV, AND OTHER PREDATORY VEHICLES TO MAINTAIN HER PERFECT BALANCE.

BLAB BLAH!
BLAB!
BLAH!

WHUMP!

CAR AND DRIVER CAN ADAPT RAPIDLY TO THEIR ENVIRONMENT.

SUPER

TOTAL
49.0¢
2.30 GAL
06 031
LEAD GAS
0104
OCTANE

$2.99 A GALLON? WE'LL REPEAL THE GAS TAX!

THEY HAVE ONLY ONE KNOWN ENEMY IN ALL OF NATURE: THE RADIATION-EMITTING CELL PHONE.

TROUBLETOWN

BY LLOYD DANGLE

DAY 0 THE EGG IS PUNCTURED WITH A SHARP NEEDLE AND A SPERM IS INJECTED.

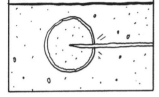

DAY 1 THE BABY HAS CLEAVED INTO TWO CELLS. ANTI-ABORTION PROTESTORS FORM A HUMAN CHAIN AROUND THE EGG SAC.

DAY 2 THE BABY WILL FEND OFF RESEARCHERS; CLONED BABIES WILL BEGIN TO SHOW THEIR FIRST ABNORMALITIES.

YOU GOING TO USE THIS?

CARNIVAL SIDE SHOW!

DAY 2 AT SEVEN CELLS, THE BABY MAKES ITS FIRST CONTACT WITH THE RAELIAN SPACESHIP.

WE COME AS FRIENDS.

DAY 3 THE BABY IS IMPLANTED IN THE MOTHER'S UTERUS AND ALREADY BEGINS TO RESENT THE CONFINEMENT.

DAY 3 THE BABY RECEIVES ITS FIRST FAX FROM A MEMBER CONGRESS REQUESTING A DONATION.

DAY 4 AT DAY FOUR, THE BABY IS ALREADY BEING FORCED TO LEARN FRENCH AND STUDY PRENATAL ALGEBRA.

DAY 5 THE INSURANCE COMPANY DEVELOPS A FLIMSY EXCUSE FOR DENYING COVERAGE.

YOU DIDN'T READ THE FINE PRINT!

DAY 6 WHILE STILL ONE-HUNDRED TIMES SMALLER THAN A POPPYSEED, THE BABY SEEKS COUNSELING.

TROUBLETOWN

BY LLOYD DANGLE

THE BABY ISN'T DUE FOR SIX MORE WEEKS, SO I'VE GOT TIME TO DO MY CARTOONS AND SHEET-ROCK THE MASTER BEDROOM!

HONEY, I THINK MY WATER BROKE.

C'MON, DON'T JOKE AROUND. GRAB A TROWEL!

5 MINUTES LATER

YOU'RE 3½ CENTIMETERS AND 90% EFFACED!

WHAT? WE DON'T HAVE TIME TO USE ALL THOSE BREATHING TECHNIQUES WE'VE PRACTICED FOR MONTHS?!

I GOT HERE AS SOON AS I COULD. TRAFFIC WAS A NIGHTMARE.

DOCTOR SHWARZ IS OFF TODAY AND DOCTOR FENNOWITZ ISN'T PICKING UP. DON'T START PUSHING!

HI, I'M DOCTOR LOWELL. DON'T START PUSHING UNTIL I CHANGE OUT OF MY STREET DUDS.

SORRY, THIS NEXT PART IS TOO GRAPHIC EVEN FOR GRAPHIC ART!

GO GIRL!   YEAH!   WOO!

PUSH!

TROUBLETOWN

BY LLOYD DANGLE

Panel 1: IT'S TRUE WHAT THEY SAY ABOUT PARENTHOOD; IT CHANGES YOUR PERSPECTIVE ON EVERYTHING!

z z z z z z

Panel 2: I USED TO BE WORRIED ABOUT THE MISSILE SHIELD...

THAT THING WILL NEVER WORK!

MISSILE SHIELD

Panel 3: NOW I'M WORRIED ABOUT THE **NIPPLE** SHIELD!

THAT THING WILL NEVER WORK!

Panel 4: I USED TO WORRY ABOUT THE ENRON CORPORATE SCANDAL; NOW I'M WORRIED ABOUT THE **TYCO** CORPORATE SCANDAL.

CRIMINALS!

Panel 5: I USED TO READ THE PAPER COVER-TO-COVER AND OBSESS OVER EVERYTHING POLITICIANS DID.

HAW! ASHCROFT WILL MAKE THE MARIN TALIBAN PAY BECAUSE OSAMA ESCAPED!

Panel 6: NOW I'M OBSESSED WITH **REAL** CHILDISH ANTICS.

LOOK! HE JUST WINKED!

YOU'VE BEEN STARING AT HIM FOR FOUR HOURS.

Panel 7: I USED TO WORRY ABOUT MISSING MY DEADLINES; NOW I'M HAPPY IF I CAN KEEP DIAPER CONTENTS OFF THE ARTWORK.

LATE — AND POOPY!

Panel 8: I USED TO CONCERN MYSELF WITH THE PLIGHT OF THE POOR, ELDERLY AND DISPOSSESSED...

STREET SHEET?

Panel 9: NOW I'm **PRO FAMILY.**

MOVE IT, PAL! FAMILY COMING THROUGH!

CRUNCH!

TROUBLETOWN

READERS RESPOND: THEY HATE BABIES!

BY LLOYD DANGLE

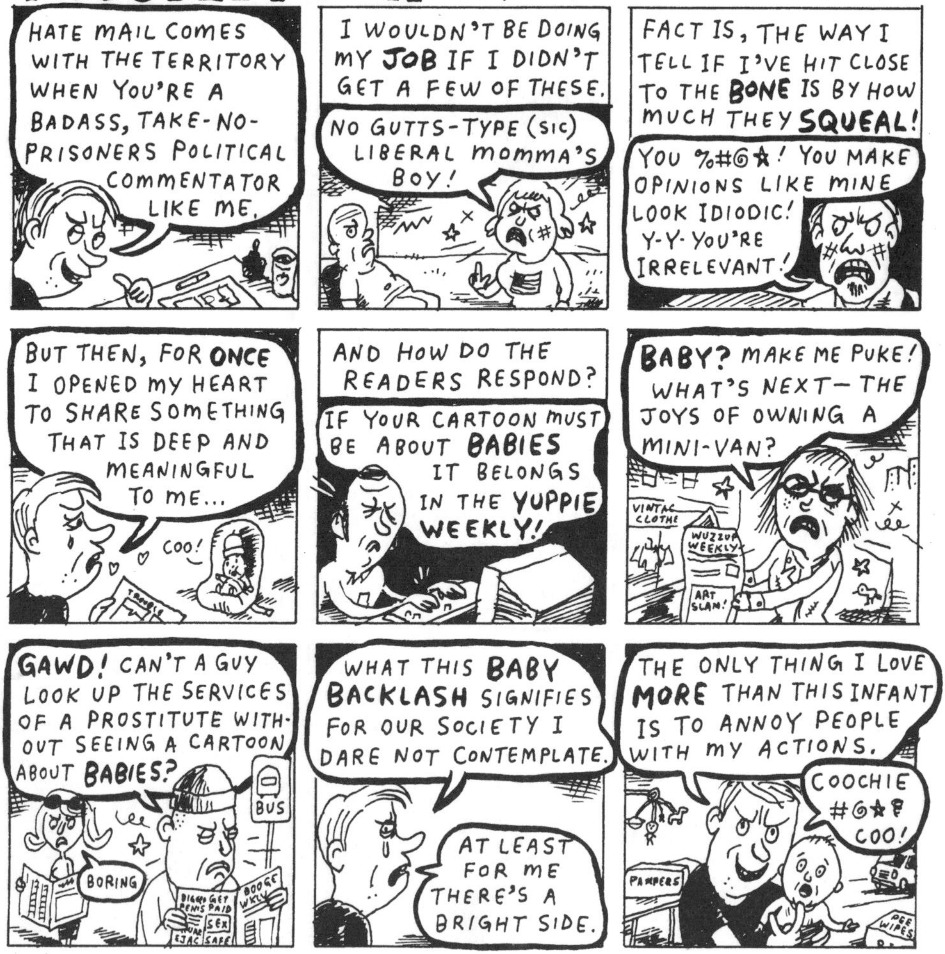
HATE MAIL COMES WITH THE TERRITORY WHEN YOU'RE A BADASS, TAKE-NO-PRISONERS POLITICAL COMMENTATOR LIKE ME.
I WOULDN'T BE DOING MY JOB IF I DIDN'T GET A FEW OF THESE.
NO GUTTS-TYPE (SIC) LIBERAL MOMMA'S BOY!
FACT IS, THE WAY I TELL IF I'VE HIT CLOSE TO THE BONE IS BY HOW MUCH THEY SQUEAL!
YOU %#@☆! YOU MAKE OPINIONS LIKE MINE LOOK IDIODIC! Y-Y-YOU'RE IRRELEVANT!
BUT THEN, FOR ONCE I OPENED MY HEART TO SHARE SOMETHING THAT IS DEEP AND MEANINGFUL TO ME...
COO!
AND HOW DO THE READERS RESPOND?
IF YOUR CARTOON MUST BE ABOUT BABIES IT BELONGS IN THE YUPPIE WEEKLY!
BABY? MAKE ME PUKE! WHAT'S NEXT—THE JOYS OF OWNING A MINI-VAN?
VINTAGE CLOTHE
WUZZUP WEEKLY
ART SLAM!
GAWD! CAN'T A GUY LOOK UP THE SERVICES OF A PROSTITUTE WITHOUT SEEING A CARTOON ABOUT BABIES?
BUS
BORING
GET PAID
SEX
BOOGE WKLY
WHAT THIS BABY BACKLASH SIGNIFIES FOR OUR SOCIETY I DARE NOT CONTEMPLATE.
AT LEAST FOR ME THERE'S A BRIGHT SIDE.
THE ONLY THING I LOVE MORE THAN THIS INFANT IS TO ANNOY PEOPLE WITH MY ACTIONS.
COOCHIE #@☆! COO!
PAMPERS
PEE WIPES

Pickleweed

BY LLOYD DANGLE

COUSIN JEREMY, I BET YOU'RE GOING TO TRY TO CONVINCE US TO MOVE OUT TO THE COUNTRY TO RAISE OUR KID, RIGHT?

NOPE.

HA!

C'MON, WHAT ABOUT HEARTLAND VALUES, NATURE, AND HOME SCHOOLING? GIVE ME THE PITCH!

THE DEER ALL HAVE IT. MAD COW DISEASE.

GOO!

DOES THAT MEAN THAT DEER ARE CANNIBALIZING EACH OTHER?

THEY DON'T KNOW WHY IT HAPPENS.

BUT ANY TIME I BAG A DEER, I MUST DON A HAZ-MAT SUIT AND BURN THE CARCASS.

THAT'S TERRIBLE.

Y'KNOW, SHOTGUN SHELLS AND ORANGE VESTS ACCOUNT FOR TWO THIRDS OF OUR ECONOMY OUT HERE.

WAH!

HEY, DON'T USE THAT MOSQUITO REPELLENT. WEST NILE ONES HAVE A RESISTANCE TO IT.

I'LL BLAST YOU.

I WAS GONNA ASK YOU TWO IF YOU HAVE ANY CONTACTS IN L.A. DO YOU THINK I'D STAND A CHANCE AT PLAYING A REDNECK ON TV?

UH, MAYBE.

BELL CURVE OF BELLICOSITY

WHACK!

TROUBLETOWN

SHAKESPEAREAN GOLF DRAMA

BY LLOYD DANGLE

OUR VERY PLUTOCRACY IS IN DISARRAY OVER WHETHER OR NOT TO ATTACK IRAQ!

BROTHER, I AGREE WITH SCROWCROFT!

DAMN IT, NOT DURING MY BACK-SWING!

NORMALLY, THE RULING FAMILY ACTS AS A COHESIVE, UNSHAKABLE ADVOCATE FOR THE OIL-RICH GENTRY, BUT NOW—

IT'S MOTHER AGAINST SON!

BROTHER AGAINST DAD!

IT MATTERS LITTLE TO THE ROYAL FAMILY WHAT CONGRESS THINKS, BUT WHEN FRIENDS OF THE THRONE CHALLENGE THE YOUNG KING:

JAMES BAKER III HATH BETRAYED YOU!

SNIFF! HE WAS LIKE A WET NURSE TO ME.

DEAR MOTHER, WHY DOES THE FAMILY FORSAKE ME?

YOU MUST SEE YOUR FATHER.

AND TAKE THIS!

WAH! I THOUGHT ENDING SADDAM'S REIN WOULD PLEASE YOU, FATHER!

SILENCE! STAND THERE AND TEND TO THINE FLAG!

KING FAHAD, WHAT TAKES THE BUSHES SO LONG TO PUTT OUT?

I DUNNO BUT I CAN WAIT NO LONGER! LET'S PRAY I DON'T BEAN ONE OF THEM!

TROUBLETOWN'S E-Z GUIDE TO FRIENDS & FOES IN THE REGION

BY LLOYD DANGLE

THE NORTHERN ALLIANCE HATES THE TALIBAN

HELP US FIND OSAMA.

OK.

THE NORTHERN ALLIANCE AND TALIBAN FOUGHT SIDE-BY-SIDE AGAINST THE USSR

POW! POW! POW!

THE UNITED STATES HATED THE USSR

WE'LL HELP YOU WIN, OSAMA.

OK.

NOW THE UNITED STATES AND RUSSIA ARE FRIENDS

HELP US FIND OSAMA, PUTIN.

OK

RUSSIA ARMS THE NORTHERN ALLIANCE

ENJOY.

THE TALIBAN LIKES OSAMA

WE'LL HELP YOU WIN THE JIHAD.

OK.

THE UNITED STATES LIKED THE TALIBAN'S WAR ON DRUGS

WOW!

THE NORTHERN ALLIANCE SELLS BLACK TAR HEROIN

AMERICAN TEEN

AFGHANI PEOPLE HAVE NOTHING TO EAT BUT BOILED GRASS

THE NORTHERN ALLIANCE LIKED SADDAM IN THE GULF WAR

U.S.A.

THE UNITED STATES LIKED SADDAM IN THE WAR AGAINST IRAN

WE'LL HELP YOU WIN.

OK.

THE UNITED STATES HATES SADDAM EVER SINCE THE WAR ON KUWAIT

HELP US FIND SADDAM

IRAN'S SHIITE MUSLIMS HATE THE TALIBAN'S SUNNI MUSLIMS

FRAUD! INFIDEL!

IRAN HELPS THE NORTHERN ALLIANCE EVEN THOUGH IT HATES THEM TOO

BUNCHA ☆#% HAZARAS!

EVEN THE MEMBERS OF THE NORTHERN ALLIANCE CAN BARELY STAND EACH OTHER

TAJIK! UZBEK!

THE UNITED STATES LIKES ISRAEL THE MOST

TROUBLETOWN

BY LLOYD DANGLE

PHASE TWO IN THE WAR ON TERRORISM:

FINISH OFF THE TALIBAN WITH GROUND TROOPS; EXPAND THE WAR TO IRAQ. (SADDAM HO!)

PHASE THREE IN THE WAR ON TERRORISM:

EXPAND THE WAR TO IRAN, YEMEN, CUBA, LIBYA AND NORTH KOREA; GIVE THE RICH ANOTHER TAX CUT.

PHASE FOUR IN THE WAR ON TERRORISM:

FERRET OUT TERRORISTS IN THE GENERAL ACCOUNTING OFFICE; EXPAND INTO SPAIN.

PHASES 5, 6, AND 7 IN THE WAR ON TERRORISM: GET BUSH RE-ELECTED WITH A TAX CUT AND DECISIVE VICTORY AGAINST TERROR IN THE NETHERLANDS.

PHASES EIGHT AND NINE IN THE WAR ON TERRORISM:

GIVE FRIENDLY NATIONS GIFT CERTIFICATES TO NORTHROP GRUMMAN.

(Sale!)

PHASE NINE-AND-A-HALF IN THE WAR ON TERRORISM: UNCOVER JOHN McCAIN'S TERROR CONNECTIONS; UNDO ALL CAMPAIGN FINANCE REFORMS.

DAMN IT!

PHASE TEN IN THE WAR ON TERRORISM: CUT TAXES FOR THE TOP .05% WEALTHIEST; INFORM CONGRESS OF THE LATEST RAIDS.

IT'S A POST-IT. / BERMUDA, CHINA AND PORTUGAL!

PHASES 11 THROUGH 15 IN THE WAR ON TERRORISM: GET **REALLY** SERIOUS ABOUT FINDING OSAMA; ATTACK ALL OF THE COUNTRIES WITH NAMES THAT END IN "ISTAN" FOR A SECOND TIME!

PHASE SIXTEEN IN THE WAR ON TERRORISM:

GET BUSH ELECTED TO A THIRD TERM!

BUSH GIULIANI

AH NEED MORE TIME TO DEFEAT EVIL—AND CUT YOUR TAXES!

Harry Rumsfeld

BY LLOYD DANGLE

TROUBLETOWN

BY LLOYD DANGLE

COLIN POWELL'S MOST IMPORTANT DIPLOMATIC MISSION:

MR. SHARON, THE PRESIDENT IS VERY UPSET WITH YOU. VERY, VERY, VERY UPSET.

FIRST, "WAR ON TERRORISM," THAT'S OUR LINE!

WE THOUGHT OF IT FIRST!

IT'S **OUR** WAR!

NO, IT'S NOT!

OKAY, WE'VE FAILED TO REACH ACCORD ON THAT. BUT YOU **KNEW** ABOUT OUR PLAN, OPERATION ENDURING PIPELINE, TO TAKE OUT SADDAM!

SO WHAT?

YOU SHOULD'VE WAITED! NOW JORDAN, EGYPT, SYRIA, IRAN, LEBANON, PAKISTAN AND SAUDI ARABIA HAVE ALL DENIED US AIR SPACE!

ISRAEL WAITS FOR NO ONE.

CHENEY HAS ALREADY SELECTED THE SECRET BOARD OF EXECUTIVES WHO WILL MANAGE THE "POST-SADDAM TRANSITION." SOME ALREADY HAVE THEIR MISTRESSES AND GOLF CLUBS ON THE GROUND!

OH.

ARE YOU TELLING ME, THAT'S EXACTLY WHAT I'M TELLING YOU, SIR.

DON'T MESS WITH TEXAS?

OKAY, I'LL PULL BACK.

MY MISSION IS A SUCCESS.

TROUBLETOWN

BY LLOYD DANGLE

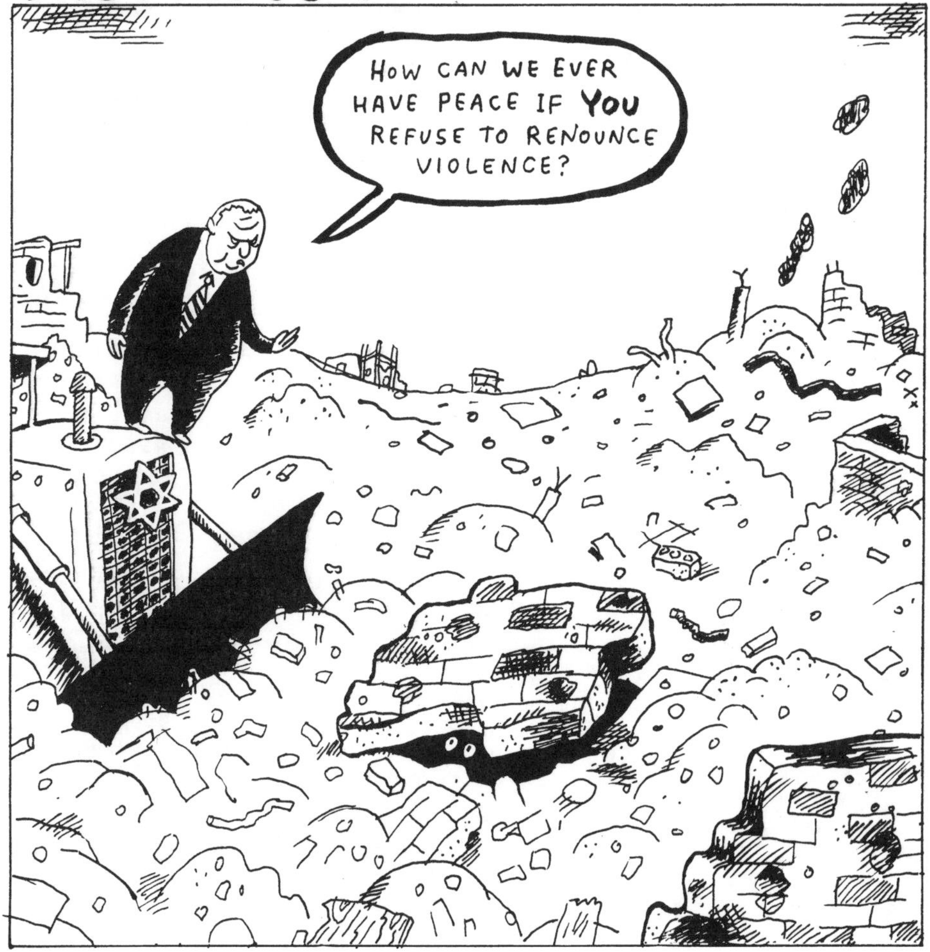

HOW CAN WE EVER HAVE PEACE IF YOU REFUSE TO RENOUNCE VIOLENCE?

TROUBLETOWN

BY LLOYD DANGLE

Panel 1: SECRETARY RUMSFELD, WHAT WOULD BE THE COST OF GOING TO WAR WITH IRAQ?

CHAIRMAN

Panel 2: THE QUESTION IS, WHAT WOULD BE THE COST OF **NOT** GOING TO WAR WITH IRAQ?!

WE CAN'T AFFORD TO FIND OUT!

Panel 3: HOW LONG WILL A WAR WITH IRAQ TAKE?

Panel 4: THIS MUCH IS CLEAR: THE LONGER WE WAIT TO ATTACK, THE LONGER IT'LL BE UNTIL WE CAN DECLARE VICTORY.

Panel 5: IS THERE A SMOKING GUN THAT PROVES SADDAM HAS WEAPONS OF MASS DESTRUCTION?

Panel 6: IF A GUN SMOKES IN THE FOREST AND NOBODY SEES IT, MILITARY EXPERTS ASSURE ME THAT IT STILL SMOKES, MADAM!

Panel 7: IS BUSH GOING TO ATTACK SADDAM AS AN ATTEMPT TO DIVERT PUBLIC ATTENTION FROM HIS FAILURE TO CATCH OSAMA?

Panel 8: DID IT EVER OCCUR TO YOU THAT MAYBE OSAMA'S FAILURE TO GET CAUGHT WAS AN ATTEMPT TO DIVERT ATTENTION AWAY FROM SADDAM?

HUH?

Panel 9: DID YOU GET ANY OF THAT?

NOT A WORD, BUT I'LL GIVE BUSH MY VOTE ANYWAY.

ME TOO! A LACK OF **SADDAM SYMPATHY** HAS NEVER COST ANYBODY AN ELECTION!

TROUBLETOWN

BY LLOYD DANGLE

BUSH'S UNSMOKING GUNS! LOOKS LIKE A REGULAR SMOKING GUN ↓ BUT ON CLOSER OBSERVATION, IT'S REALLY AN AIR FRESHENER!

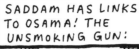

SADDAM HAS LINKS TO OSAMA! THE UNSMOKING GUN: OSAMA AND SADDAM HAVE NEVER BEEN ALLIES. ↓

SADDAM— YOU INFIDEL! I WILL NEVER DO TERROR W/ YOU! / YEVAS, OSAMA

SADDAM WON'T LET THE UN INSPECTORS IN! THE UNSMOKING GUN:

I WILL LET THE UN INSPECTORS IN.

SADDAM WON'T LET INSPECTORS IN, PART II. THE UNSMOKING GUN: WILL YOU LET 'EM IN UNDER THESE CONDITIONS? HA! HA! DIDN'T THINK SO!

CHENEY'S CONDITIONS

TONY BLAIR HAS A DOSSIER PROVING SADDAM HAS WEAPONS. THE UNSMOKING GUN: DUBYA GAVE HIM A MATCHING DOSSIER VALAISE AND BOOTS! → SPIFFY!

SADDAM LIES! THE INTERNATIONAL ATOMIC ENERGY COMMISSION REPORTED THAT IRAQ IS SIX MONTHS AWAY FROM HAVING NUCLEAR WEAPONS! INT'NL ATOMIC NERGY MISSIUM / ACTUALLY, WE NEVER REPORTED THAT.

WEAPONS EXPERTS ARE IMPRESSED BY THE SOPHISTICATION OF IRAQ'S STOCKPILE! HA! HA! IRAQ'S CAPABILITIES ARE A JOKE!

NOW ISRAEL HAS A GOOD NUCLEAR WEAPONS PROGRAM!

INTERNATIONAL SUPPORT CONTINUES TO GROW WITH EACH REVELATION! DID I MENTION I HAVE A DOSSIER?

FORMER STATESMEN ALL AGREE THAT PRE-EMPTIVE ATTACK IS A GREAT NEW POLICY! I'M PRACTICALLY A WAR CRIMINAL AND EVEN I WOULDN'T DO THAT.

← KISSINGER

TROUBLETOWN

EXCEPT FOR THOSE WHOSE INVESTMENTS ARE TIED TO OIL AND WAR, THERE'S LITTLE SUPPORT ANYWHERE IN THE WORLD FOR WAR WITH IRAQ.

WE DON'T LOOK AT POLLS...

WE LOOK AT OUR PORTFOLIOS!

WITH ELECTIONS COMING, NOW WOULD BE THE TIME FOR LEADING DEMOCRATS TO SHOW THEIR METTLE, RIGHT?

ASK ANYBODY, MY NICKNAME HAS ALWAYS BEEN "**REGIME CHANGE**" GEPHARDT!

HEH! HEH!

EVEN THOUGH I DON'T NORMALLY LIKE TO DO IT, THE NATION SOMETIMES CALLS ON US TO BAKE COOKIES WHILE THE U.N. CHALLENGES THE PRESIDENT'S UNCHECKED POWER.

W-W-WHEN UNILATERAL WAR COULD BREAK OUT AT ANY MINUTE, WE MUST STAND WITH OUR PRESIDENT.

BUT I'LL THROW A MAJOR HUFFY ANY— REPEAT— **ANY** TIME HE INSULTS US ON TV.

SECRET INTELLIGENCE MADE ME SUPPORT THE PRESIDENT.

MY BLOW DRYER TOLD ME TO DO IT.

HELL NO! THIS WAR RESOLUTION IS OUTRAGEOUS!

WHAT'S SENATOR BYRD UP TO?

DON'T WORRY, HIS PRESIDENTIAL AMBITIONS DON'T HAVE ANY WINGS!

STUPID! ASININE!

TROUBLETOWN

CATCHPHRASES FOR THE NEW REPUBLICAN REVOLUTION!

BY LLOYD DANGLE

IT'S THE TERROR, STUPID!	**A THOUSAND POINTS OF ASHCROFT**	**CONTRACT TO DRILL**	**MORNING IN AMERICA WITH NO ACCESS TO A DOCTOR**
EXTREME GINGRICH!	**IF YOU CAN'T DO THE TIME, DON'T LOOK MIDDLE EASTERN**	**SCREW THE POOR MORE 'TILL '04**	**WAKE UP AND SMELL THE PRO-LIFE SUPREME COURT!**
ZERO TOLERANCE OF PELOSI	**LET A MILLION ARCTIC DERRICKS BLOOM!**	**THE DESTITUTE RETIREE REVOLUTION!**	**ALL THAT AND A BAG OF WHOOPASS!**

WHACK!

HE'S BACK!

TASTY!

OUCH!

WILL KNIT FOR FOOD

TROUBLETOWN

BY LLOYD DANGLE

Panel 1: PRE-EMPTIVE ATTACK IS SUPPOSEDLY A BRAND NEW STRATEGY MADE NECESSARY BY TERRORISM...

WE MUSTN'T WAIT FOR ANOTHER 9-11! WE MUST ACT FIRST!

AND DOMINATE THE GLOBE.

AND GRAB THE OIL.

Panel 2: BUT ACTUALLY, DICK CHENEY AND PAUL WOLFOWITZ CAME UP WITH THE IDEA WAY BACK IN 1989!

WE MUSTN'T WAIT FOR ANOTHER SOVIET UNION TO FORM...

GLOBAL DOMINATION.

THAT'S SOME HEAVY DOO-DOO!

OIL!

OUR PLAN

Panel 3: COLIN POWELL PITCHED IN TOO.

NOW THAT THERE IS NO SOVIET THREAT, WE MUST BE PREPARED TO FIGHT TWO WARS SIMULTANEOUSLY!

AND STRIKE FIRST.

AND GLOBAL DOMINATION.

AND OIL.

Panel 4: THEN THERE WAS AN EIGHT YEAR BREAK,

CLINTON'S AN IDIOT! TWO WARS SIMULTANEOUSLY!

ATTACK FIRST!

GLOBAL DOM!

OIL!

DID NOT.. HAVE SEX...

Panel 5: BUT WHEN DUBYA WAS MADE PRESIDENT, POWELL, CHENEY, AND WOLFOWITZ GOT ANOTHER CHANCE!

THIS PLAN IS OLD AND MESSY. UNACCEPTABLE!

WAR²!

ATTK4OIL!

GLOBDOM!

OUR PLAN

Panel 6: SO, JUST WHEN IT APPEARED THAT THE INTERNATIONAL-LAW-VIOLATING PLAN WAS DEAD...

OSAMA TO THE RESCUE!

HELP ME FIND THE PLAN, WOLFIE!

GLOBDOM!

TROUBLETOWN

BY LLOYD DANGLE

AS IF "THE LEFT" NEEDED ANY MORE PROBLEMS, TURMOIL HAS ERUPTED AMONG THE INTELLECTUALS OVER WAR WITH IRAQ!

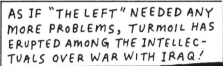

PAUL BINDLE! HOW **DARE** YOU SHOW UP AT **MY** BLEEKER STREET COFFEE SHOP!

?

YOU OUGHTA' BE ASHAMED OF YOUR-SELF AFTER LAST WEEK'S COLUMN IN TIKKUN!

YOUR ARTICLE IN THE NEW LEFT OBSERVER WAS THE SAME UNCONVINCING CLAPTRAP YOU'VE BEEN PEDDLING FOR YEARS!

HOW YOU COULD **PRETEND** THAT WAR WITH SADDAM WILL BRING ABOUT **DEMOCRACY** IS ABSURD!

HOW YOU COULD **IGNORE** SADDAM'S LETHAL USE OF BIOLOGICAL WEAPONS IS **APPALLING!**

KATHA POLLITT WAS RIGHT ABOUT YOU ON THE LETTERS PAGE OF THE NATION, YOU'RE A WOLFOWITZ IN SHEEP'S CLOTHING!

ALEX COCKBURN HAD YOU PEGGED WHEN HE SAID YOU'RE A NOAM CHOMSKY WANNABE!

HOW DARE YOU QUESTION MY LEFTIST CREDEN-TIALS, DONALD RUMSFELD-LITE!

I'M MORE LEFT THAN YOU'LL EVER BE, PROGRESSIVE POLLYWOG!

PHONY NEOCON!

DESPOT APOLOGIST!

MEANWHILE, IN THE OTHER 99.6% OF AMERICA:

FROM HIS HAIRCUT, I'D SAY HE'S A LIBERAL.

ME TOO.

LET'S KILL HIM.

TROUBLETOWN

BY LLOYD DANGLE

FOR CHRISTMAS, NORTH KOREA SENT YEMEN A BOX OF **SCUDS**.

SCUDS! I LOVE THEM!

YOU CAN RETURN THEM IF THEY'RE TOO SMALL.

CANADA GAVE TURKEY SOME STINGERS, FRANCE SENT SOME PLANES TO PAKISTAN, AND EVERYBODY PITCHED IN TO SEND WEAPONS TO SUDAN, ANGOLA, AND THE CONGO!

THERE WOULD BE NO CHRISTMAS AT ALL WITHOUT YOU!

BRITAIN SENT TANKS TO INDONESIA, BELARUS SENT SHOULDER-FIRED SOVIET SA-7's TO LIBYA.

YOU SHOULDN'T HAVE!

BE CAREFUL NOT TO POINT THAT AT ANY COMMERCIAL JETLINERS.

THE UNITED STATES SENT ISRAEL A DIFFERENT WEAPON SYSTEM FOR EACH DAY OF CHANUKAH!

HOT DAMN! THE ONE WITH THE **LONGBOW RADAR SYSTEM**!

BUT IN BAGHDAD THERE ARE NO PRESENTS UNDER SADDAM'S TREE.

NOT EVEN ENOUGH SARIN TO GAS A MOUSE!

SOB!

WHY ARE SOME COUNTRIES LEFT OUT OF THE TRADITIONAL GLOBAL GIFT-GIVING RITUAL?

BECAUSE IT'S ONLY FOR US WHO ARE **NON-HOSTILE**!

TROUBLETOWN

THE DIFFERENCE BETWEEN IRAQ & NORTH KOREA AT-A-GLANCE!

SADDAM IS RUTHLESS, COLD-BLOODED, AND DOESN'T VALUE HUMAN LIFE — LIKE WE DO.

 KIM IL JONG IS RUTHLESS, COLD-BLOODED, AND DOESN'T VALUE HUMAN LIFE — BUT IN A NICE WAY!

 RIGHT ACROSS THE STREET!
SADDAM COULD HIT **ISRAEL** WITH A NUCLEAR BOMB OR A SCUD FULL OF NERVE GAS!

WITHOUT HIS GLASSES, KIM IL JONG WOULD BE LUCKY TO HIT THE SIDE OF A CHINESE BARN WITH A CLUSTER BOMB!
HEY! WATCH IT! PING!

SADDAM: EVIL EVERY DAY OF THE WEEK, ALL DAY LONG.

 KIM IL JONG: EVERY DAY IS AN EVIL HAIR DAY.

 POOF
IN IRAQ, KURDS ARE INNOCENT PEOPLE TO BE SPRAYED WITH POISON GAS.

IN NORTH KOREA, KURDS ARE THE LUMPS FOUND IN COTTAGE CHEESE.
SURE WISH I HAD SOME. SMALL KURD LITE N' LIVELY

SADDAM: TOTALLY UNPREDICTABLE.
UH, **NO!** MY PALACE SOCK DRAWER IS **OFF LIMITS!** GIVE ME A COUPLE OF DAYS. NO WMD'S IN THERE!

KIM IL JONG: TOTALLY UNPREDICTABLE.
WE'RE RENOVATING OUR NUCLEAR REACTOR TO BECOME A GIANT KARAOKE DISCO!

 GET OFF MY BORE HOLE! VACATE MY WELL HEAD!
THE HUSSEINS AND THE BUSHES HAVE THE SAME FAMILY BUSINESS!

SUV'S DON'T RUN ON KIM CHEE.

CONTRAPOSE OF
CONTENTEDNESS

TROUBLETOWN

BY LLOYD DANGLE

DAMN IT! WHO'S OUT HERE?!

FREEZE OR I'LL SHOOT!

WHOA, HI FRANK. FOR A SECOND I THOUGHT YOU WERE COMMITTING SUICIDE BY POLICE!

HA! HA! HA!

HEH!

HEH! HEH!

HI KEN, I THOUGHT I MIGHT HAVE TO **KILL** YOU! WHAT'S UP?

IT'S ABOUT YOUR SON. HE WROTE A DISTURBING HAIKU AT SCHOOL TODAY AND HE'S BEEN SUSPENDED.

MY WIFE BETTER HEAR THIS.

WAS HE ALIENATED AND FULL OF RAGE LIKE THAT GIRL WHO WAS ARRESTED FOR HER CERAMICS PROJECT?

WORSE.

THE KID BELIEVES IN THE THOROUGHLY DISCREDITED NOTION THAT TAKING AWAY GUNS WOULD STOP ALL THESE SCHOOL SHOOTINGS!

POLICE

I READ THE POEM MYSELF AND I NEARLY THREW UP.

HE'S NEVER TAKEN TO GUNS LIKE A NORMAL CHILD! MAYBE SOME SERIOUS TIME AT THE VIDEO ARCADE WILL STRAIGHTEN HIM OUT.

IT'S YOUR FAULT!

NO GUNS

TROUBLETOWN

BY LLOYD DANGLE

WITH THIS NEW WIRELESS TRACKING TECHNOLOGY I CAN MONITOR THE WHERABOUTS OF MY GIRLFRIEND AT ALL TIMES!

TRACK ANYONE

THIS WAY I'LL KNOW IF SHE'S CHEATING ON ME.

ZIP!

OKAY, SHE'S AT HER OFFICE...

SHE SPENDS A LOT OF TIME IN HER CUBICLE. I WONDER IF SHE'S GETTING IT ON WITH HER CO-WORKER, MELVIN.

BEEP!

OKAY, SHE'S ON THE MOVE... NO DOUBT SLIPPING AWAY TO AN INTIMATE TRYSTING LOCATION!

CHIPS

NOW SHE'S STOPPING AT THE OUTLET MALL. I HOPE SHE'S BUYING ME A PRESENT!

BOOP!

NOW SHE'S AT STROMBOLI PIZZA! SERGIO! I SHOULD'VE KNOWN **HE** WAS HER SLICE ON THE SIDE!

WOOP!

MINUTES LATER: OH, HI. WHERE'VE YOU BEEN?

GEORGE, WE NEED TO TALK.

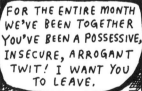

FOR THE ENTIRE MONTH WE'VE BEEN TOGETHER YOU'VE BEEN A POSSESSIVE, INSECURE, ARROGANT TWIT! I WANT YOU TO LEAVE.

IF YOU DON'T LOVE ME I DEMAND YOU RETURN THE MICROCHIP THAT I SECRETLY EMBEDDED IN YOUR SHOULDER.

TROUBLETOWN

BY LLOYD DANGLE

I RECENTLY HAD THE HONOR OF BEING INVITED TO A CONVENTION OF MEDICAL ILLUSTRATORS.

HELLO! NICE TO SEE YOU! PLEASED. HI. HELLO AGAIN!

GUEST

THE BANQUET WAS JUST LIKE THE ACADEMY AWARDS! "THE GOLDEN CUP GOES TO LAMAR MITTWOCH FOR 'GASTRO-INTESTINAL INFLAMMATION!'"

LAMAR IS GOD!! YEA! BRAVO! WOO!

IN THE CRIME CATEGORY, GEROME HOLLINGSWORTH FOR "MASSIVE TRAUMA FROM BLUNT OBJECT!"

HOORAY! DELICIOUS WHOOP!

FIG A

AFTER TWO HOURS, I REALLY NEEDED TO GET SOME AIR! "...INFECTED ABDOMINAL CAVITY WITH HEMORRHAGING PANCREAS!"

HOO! YEAH!

FIG A

BUT THEN: LLOYD DANGLE?! HOW DARE YOU COME HERE! WE KNOW WHO YOU ARE!

FELLOW

YOUR CALLOUS MOCKERY OF ANATOMY IS AN INSULT TO THE HUMAN FORM AND A STAIN ON OUR PROFESSION! THAT RENDERING OF PROJECTILE VOMIT SUCKS!

BLAGH!

TROUBLETOWN

BY LLOYD DANGLE

Panel 1: AFTER THE COURT BANNED THE EXECUTION OF MENTALLY RETARDED PEOPLE, THE DISSENTING JUSTICES HAD TO BLOW OFF SOME STEAM.

IT'S A TRAVESTY!

BAR

Panel 2: FROM A STRICT CONSTRUCTION OF THE ORIGINAL FRAMERS' INTENT, THERE'S ABSOLUTELY NO JUSTIFICATION!

I CONCUR WITH ANTONIN. YOU DA' MAN, TONY!

Panel 3: IN 1791, FOR EXAMPLE, IT WAS CONSIDERED CRUEL AND UNUSUAL TO EXECUTE AN **IDIOT** BUT IT WAS OKAY TO KILL AN **IMBECILE**.

MERCANTILE
CHAINS
GUNS
AETNA
SLAVE INSURANCE
SLAVE WHIPPING WORKSHOP 3:00
2:15 TODAY ON THE GALLOWS AN IMBECILE

Panel 4: THOSE TWO CATEGORIES COVER JUST ABOUT EVERYBODY IN THE **DEMOCRATIC PARTY** TODAY!

HAW! HAW! REHNQUIST, STOP!

HAH! HAH! HAH!

Panel 5: BUT SERIOUSLY, A LOT OF DEATH ROW INMATES WILL NOW CLAIM THEY WERE TOO RETARDED TO KNOW WHAT THEY WERE DOING!

AS A BLACK MAN, BELIEVE ME, THOSE RETARDED NEGROS KNOW A LOT MORE THAN THEY LET ON.

Panel 6: IT'S A MORAL OUTRAGE!

I HEARTILY CONCUR!

THIS LEAVES KYRGYZSTAN AS THE ONLY COUNTRY COURAGEOUS ENOUGH TO FRY THE FEEBLE-MINDED!

TROUBLETOWN

OH LOOK, THAT WOMAN IS **PREGNANT!**

WHOO!

WHOLE CANTALOUPE

YOU DON'T MIND IF I TOUCH YOUR BELLY... OOH, YEAH, THAT'S A BOY, BOYS ALWAYS MAKE YOU LUMPY HERE.

HEY!

SLAP!

PADS PADS PADS PADS

WHO'S YOUR DOULA? WHAT'S YOUR DUE DATE? HONEY, DON'T EAT THAT ROMAINE LETTUCE WHILE YOU'RE PREGNANT. IT CAN CAUSE YOUR BABY TO BE BORN WITH A HAIR LIP.

DON'T LET THE DOCTORS DRUG YOU UP! I GAVE BIRTH NATURALLY IN A FROG POND SURROUNDED BY WATERLILIES! BE SURE TO ASK FOR AN EPISIOTOMY, THEY'RE WONDERFUL!

YOU **MUST** USE CLOTH DIAPERS! YOU SHOULD BREASTFEED, BUT NOT TOO MUCH, OR YOU RISK OVARIAN CANCER. WHAT ABOUT CIRCUMCISION?

LADY, COME WITH ME.

RICE A RONI

SOUP BOX

I WANT YOU TO SIT HERE IN THE CORNER UNTIL YOU'RE READY TO BEHAVE PROPERLY IN PUBLIC.

YOU'RE NOT GOING TO DISCIPLINE YOUR CHILD THIS WAY, I HOPE!

SEAFOOD

IT COULD CAUSE PSYCHOLOGICAL PROBLEMS!

TROUBLETOWN

BY LLOYD DANGLE

DESCENDANTS OF SLAVES DESERVE REPARATIONS.

BUT THAT WAS **SO LONG** AGO! THERE AREN'T ANY ADEQUATE RECORDS OF WHO THE SLAVES WERE!

ACTUALLY, HERE AT THE MUSEUM OF INSURANCE, WE HAVE THE RECORDS OF EVERY SLAVEOWNER POLICY ISSUED BETWEEN 1790 AND 1860!

MOST SLAVE OWNERS WERE BLACK, Y'KNOW.

MY GOD, I NEVER KNEW THAT MY FAMILY WAS AUCTIONED AT SHREVEPORT, LOUISIANA!

LOOK, I DON'T DISPUTE THAT SLAVERY WAS HORRENDOUS, BUT IT'S WATER UNDER THE BRIDGE! OTHERWISE WE'D HAVE TO PAY INDIANS TOO!

BESIDES, THE — **HUH?** HEY, I'VE GOT TO LEAVE, EXCUSE ME.

ARE YOU HERE TO JOIN THE CLASS ACTION SUIT?

YOU BET! GREAT GRANDDAD'S SLAVE WAS EMANCIPATED AND G☆#% ALLSTATE DEFAULTED ON THE CLAIM!

DAMN INSURANCE COMPANIES!

TROUBLETOWN — NEIGHBORHOOD PRIEST PATROL — BY LLOYD DANGLE

TROUBLETOWN

BY LLOYD DANGLE

HI FRANK, IS THIS OUR SUSPECT?

YEAH, HE'S UNAWARE THAT WE'RE PEERING OUT AT HIM THROUGH HIS COMPUTER SCREEN.

CLIFF FIGBY, AGE 34, SINGLE, CHECKS HIS EMAIL 41 TIMES A DAY, RUNS ON A WINDOWS 95 OPERATING SYSTEM, BOUGHT A PAIR OF RUBBER RAIN BOOTS LAST TUESDAY.

HE FITS THE PROFILE.

LIVES ALONE, RENTS, WEARS BOXER SHORTS. NONE OF HIS SENT MAIL INDICATES THAT THE "LOVE, mom" VIRUS CAME FROM HIM.

KEEP CHECKING, I FEEL LUCKY.

2 HOURS LATER: HIS CHECKBOOK BALANCES! HIS CHAT ROOM POSTS ARE CLEAN! I POSED AS A YOUNG GIRL BUT HE WOULDN'T TAKE THE BAIT!

KEEP DIGGING!

6 HOURS LATER:

DAMN IT! THIS FIGBY IS A DEAD END!

I GIVE UP!

SORRY FOR THE INCONVENIENCE. YOU CAN HAVE YOUR CHAIR BACK.

NO PROBLEM. THE CONSUMER DATA TELLS ME HE'S A PRIME CANDIDATE TO BUY A CABLE TV DESCRAMBLER!

TROUBLETOWN

BY LLOYD DANGLE

LUKE FRESH REPORTING FROM A COMMUNITY GRIPPED WITH NAKED SHRIEKING TERROR!

THE PLAIN ORDINARY-NESS OF THE PLACE BELIES THE FACT THAT THERE'S A **KILLER** AMONG US!

I COULD BE IN THE CROSSHAIRS AT THIS VERY MOMENT, THE VERY SAME GUN TRAINED ON MY PERFECTLY-COIFFED HEAD!

WHAT KIND OF BULLETS DOES THE SNIPER USE? ONES JUST LIKE THIS.

REAL SNIPERS HATE THE FACT THAT WE CALL THIS CREEP A SNIPER. THEY INSIST HE'S A BEDWETTING SCUMBAG AND THAT REAL SNIPERS ARE COOL.

HOW DOES THE SNIPER ACT? IS HE A TERRORIST OR JUST A REGULAR GUY WITH A DARK SECRET?

WHAT WOULD HE BE WEARING? WHAT KIND OF SHOES? HOW WOULD HE CONCEAL THE GRASS STAINS ON HIS KNEES?

HE'S PROBABLY VERY INTELLIGENT. DOCTOR HUGH HELLMAN HAS DEVELOPED A PSYCHO-LOGICAL PROFILE.

THIS GUY REALLY GETS OFF ON BEING TALKED ABOUT ON TV. IN OTHER WORDS, HE COULD BE ANYBODY!

TROUBLETOWN

BY LLOYD DANGLE

SHOULD WE HAVE ZERO TOLERANCE, PONTIFF?

WHAT'S THAT?! SOME KIND OF CAR FINANCING? I **OWN** MY VEHICLE!

HE'S OLD!

FOR THE FIRST TIME EVER, THE FBI AND THE CLERGY HAVE LAUNCHED A CO-INVESTIGATION!

IN ORDER TO SOLVE THE SEX ABUSE SCANDAL WE'LL NEED TO EXAMINE ALL YOUR RECORDS.

OKAY. GOING HOW FAR BACK?

AS FAR AS THEY GO!

THESE MANUSCRIPTS WERE PENNED BY MONKS IN THE 13TH CENTURY.

I HOPE THEY WERE CAPPUCINO MONKS! HAH! HAH!

SPLOSH!

BINGO! I'M GOING TO RUN THE DNA ON THIS PIECE OF SAINT JOHN THE BAPTIST!

MONTHS OF POLICE WORK BY DOZENS OF AGENTS AND BISHOPS AND MILLIONS OF DOLLARS LATER:

WE'VE STOPPED INVESTIGATING, HOLY FATHER...

GOOD! TOO MUCH OF THAT WILL MAKE YOU BLIND!

WHO IS ULTIMATELY TO BLAME FOR THE SCANDAL IN THE CHURCH?

OSAMA BIN LADEN.

WOMEN AND HOMOSEXUALS.

TROUBLETOWN

BY LLOYD DANGLE

THIS YEAR'S BOARD OF EDUCATION HEARING ON SCIENCE STANDARDS FOR THE SCHOOLS HAS A NEW COMBATANT.

THE LORD MADE PEOPLE OUT OF CLAY!

PEOPLE EVOLVED FROM ALGAE OVER BILLIONS OF YEARS.

I HAVE A **NEW** IDEA!

PEOPLE EVOLVED, SURE. THE FOSSIL RECORD IS VALID, WE JUST BELIEVE THAT AN ENTITY WAS THERE MAKING DESIGN DECISIONS!

GOD IS **NOT** AN INTERIOR DECORATOR!

JUNK SCIENCE!

WE'RE NOT SAYING **WHO** THE INTELLIGENT DESIGNER IS, IT MAY EVEN BE A **DESIGN FIRM**, BUT NATURE IS JUST TOO PERFECT TO BE NATURAL!

ACADEMIC CHARLATAN!

UNWITTING TOOL OF SATAN!

I'VE BEEN COMING TO THESE HEARINGS FOR YEARS BUT YOU STILL IGNORE THE VAST EVIDENCE OF OUR EXTRA-TERRESTRIAL ORIGINS!

US PISCES PEOPLE CAME FROM ATLANTIS!

TRUE

GOSH, THIS DEBATE IS TOO HOT FOR US STATE BUREAUCRATS TO TACKLE. I MOVE THAT WE GIVE EQUAL TIME TO ALL THESE VIEWS IN THE SCHOOLS' CURRICULUM!

SO MOVED!

I SECOND!

NEXT SEPTEMBER

HAVE YOU SEEN THE **SIZE** OF THE 6TH GRADE SCIENCE BOOK? I WANNA BE HELD BACK!

EVER SINCE MY BROTHER ENTERED 6TH GRADE HE SEES A SHRINK, A RABBI, AND A PALM READER!

COKE

TROUBLE TOWN'S E-Z ABC's OF FEAR!

AIRBORNE ANTHRAX, AIRPLANES, ATTY. GENERAL ASHCROFT, AMERICA'S MOST WANTED...	BAGGAGE, BIO-LOGICAL WEAPONS, BARBERSHOPS, BRIDGES, BUSH.. 	CHEMICAL WAR-HEADS, CHENEY, CODE RED, CODE ORANGE, CODE YELLOW, BLUE... 	DIRTY BOMBS, DENTIST'S OFFICES, THE DEVIL, ENEMY COMBATANTS... 
EVILDOERS, E COLI, ENVELOPES, FLIGHT SCHOOLS, THE FRENCH... 	GARDEN VARIETY ANTHRAX, GAS ATTACKS, GROCERY STORES, GERMS.. 	HARD TARGETS, HEALTH CLUBS, HAM SANDWICHES, THE INTERNET... 	ILLEGAL ALIENS, IDENTITY THEFT, ICE RINKS, IN JAIL BY ACCIDENT... 
KRISPY KREMES, KENNELS, KIM IL JONG, LASERS, LAUNDROMATS... 	MISTAKEN MUSLIM CHARITABLE CONTRIBUTION, N. KOREAN NUKES 	NERVE GAS, NIGHTCLUBS, OVERHEAD COMPARTMENTS, OSAMA.. 	PROFESSORS, PEDOPHILES, POISONED POPCORN, PATRIOT ACT... 
QAEDA, RUMSFELD, RETIREMENT, SARIN, SMALLPOX, SUBWAYS... 	SOFT TARGETS, SADDAM-TRAINED SLEEPER CELLS, TOENAIL CLIPPERS. 	URANIUM, UNDERWEAR BOMBS, VIOLENCE ON TELEVISION... 	WRONGFULLY ACCUSED, WATER SUPPLY, YANNI CONCERT, ZAMBONI. 

TETRAHEDRON OF TERROR

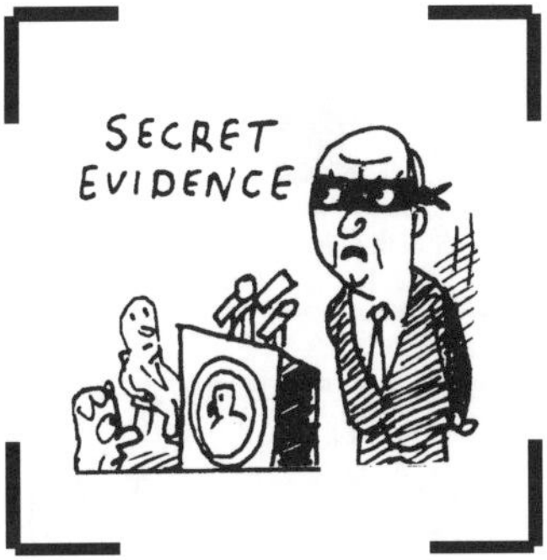
SECRET EVIDENCE

TROUBLETOWN

NINE NECESSARY STAGES

BY LLOYD DANGLE

1. SHOCK AND HORROR

2. TELEVISION OVERLOAD

HERE'S THAT HORRIBLE FOOTAGE FOR THE 296,000,000TH TIME!

UGH!

3. OVERWHELMING SADNESS

4. DISTRACTION & IRRITABILITY

I'LL TAKE THIS ONE. NO, THIS ONE! I CAN'T DECIDE!

FLAG HEADQU.

59¢

5. DEPRESSION,

SURE, I'LL GIVE UP SOME CIVIL LIBERTIES. WHAT DO I CARE?

6. PRIDE

THOSE ARE MY HEROES!

WOO!

7. PRIDE MIXED WITH UNCONTROLLABLE ANGER,

DAMN THEM!

WAVE! WAVE!

8. ANGER MIXED WITH VIOLENT FANTASY

REVENGE! **REVENGE!**

KILL!

NUKE 'EM!

9, THE RETURN OF CRITICAL THINKING

I'M STILL PROUD & ANGRY, BUT MAYBE THE ALL-OUT MILITARY ASSAULT IS A NUTTY IDEA.

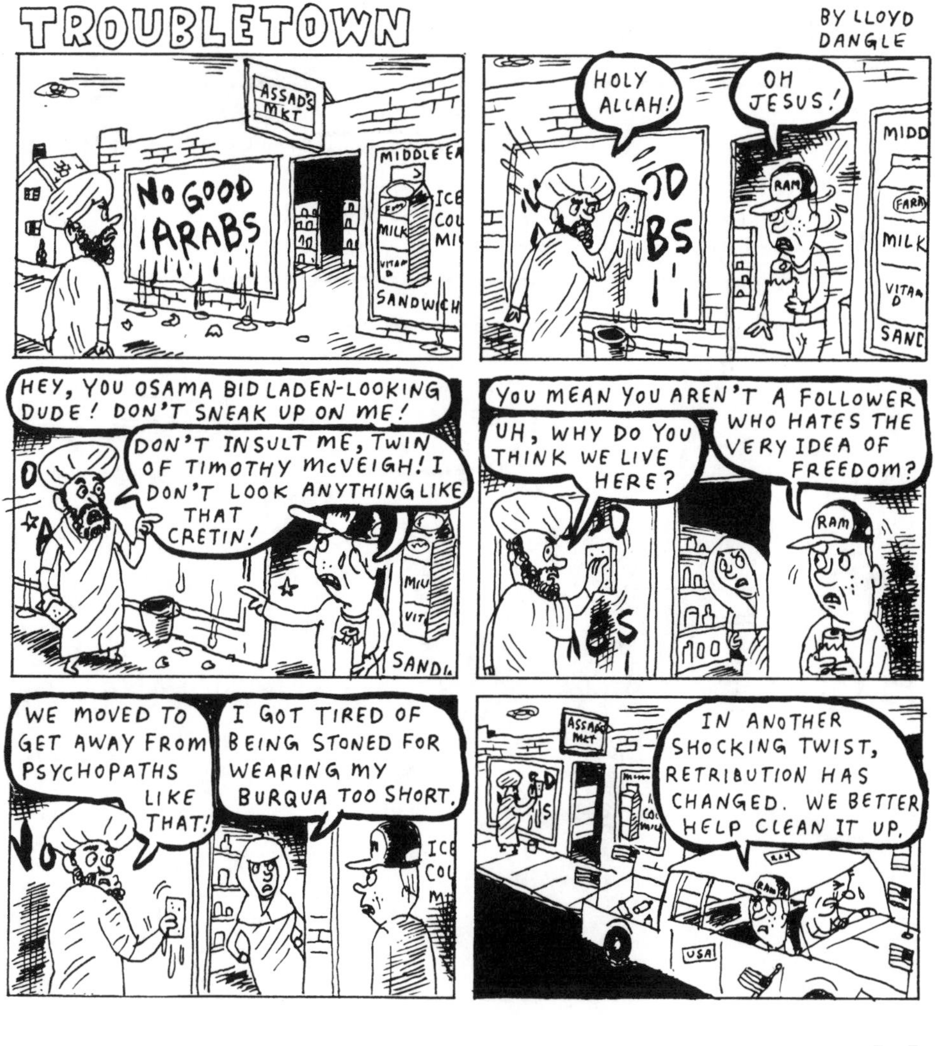
TROUBLETOWN
BY LLOYD DANGLE
ASSAD'S MKT
NO GOOD ARABS
MIDDLE EA
MILK
VITAM D
SANDWICH
HOLY ALLAH!
OH JESUS!
RAM
HEY, YOU OSAMA BID LADEN-LOOKING DUDE! DON'T SNEAK UP ON ME!
DON'T INSULT ME, TWIN OF TIMOTHY McVEIGH! I DON'T LOOK ANYTHING LIKE THAT CRETIN!
YOU MEAN YOU AREN'T A FOLLOWER WHO HATES THE VERY IDEA OF FREEDOM?
UH, WHY DO YOU THINK WE LIVE HERE?
WE MOVED TO GET AWAY FROM PSYCHOPATHS LIKE THAT!
I GOT TIRED OF BEING STONED FOR WEARING MY BURQUA TOO SHORT.
IN ANOTHER SHOCKING TWIST, RETRIBUTION HAS CHANGED. WE BETTER HELP CLEAN IT UP.
USA

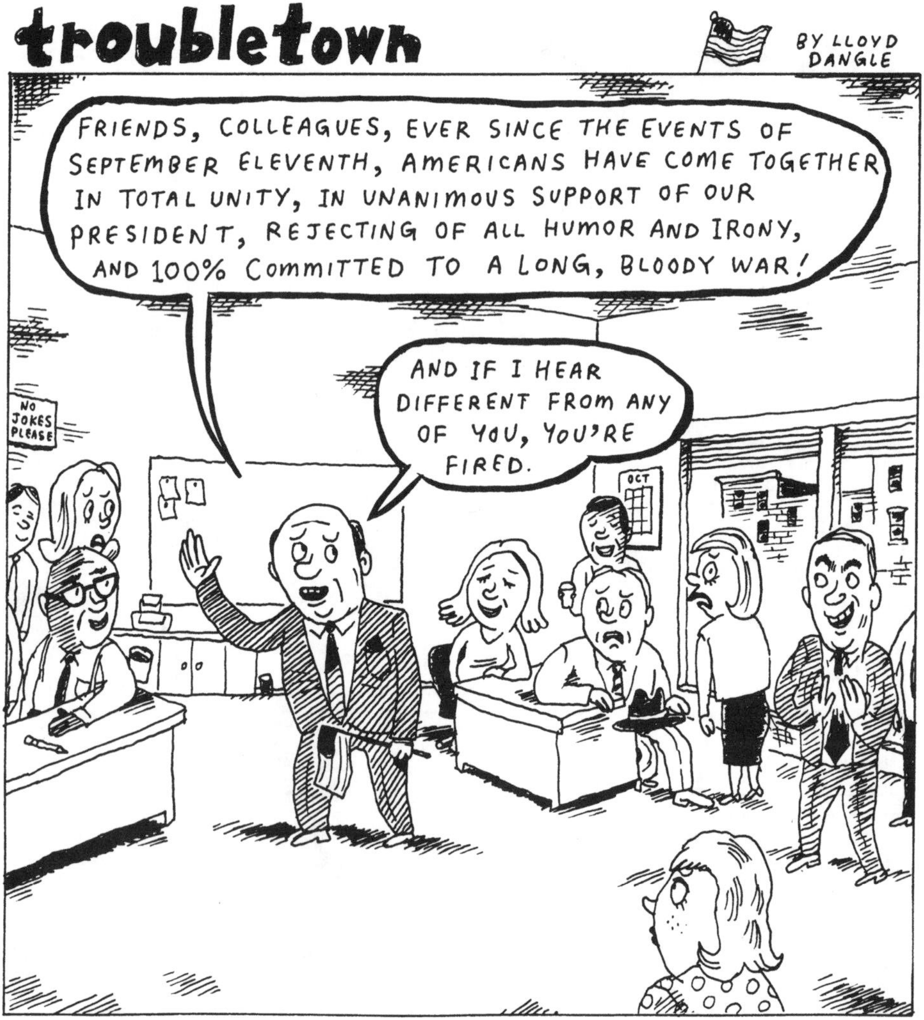
troubletown
BY LLOYD DANGLE
FRIENDS, COLLEAGUES, EVER SINCE THE EVENTS OF SEPTEMBER ELEVENTH, AMERICANS HAVE COME TOGETHER IN TOTAL UNITY, IN UNANIMOUS SUPPORT OF OUR PRESIDENT, REJECTING OF ALL HUMOR AND IRONY, AND 100% COMMITTED TO A LONG, BLOODY WAR!
AND IF I HEAR DIFFERENT FROM ANY OF YOU, YOU'RE FIRED.
NO JOKES PLEASE
OCT

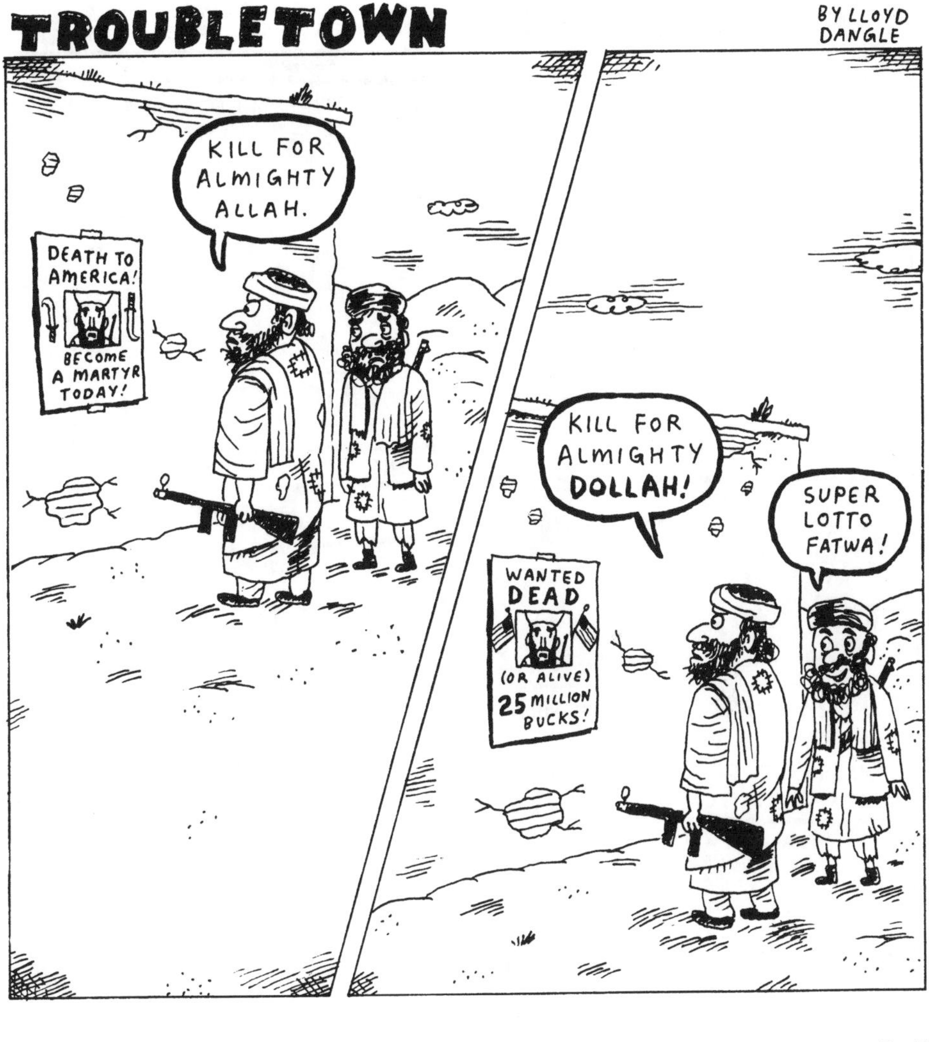
TROUBLETOWN
BY LLOYD DANGLE
KILL FOR ALMIGHTY ALLAH.
DEATH TO AMERICA! BECOME A MARTYR TODAY!
KILL FOR ALMIGHTY DOLLAH!
SUPER LOTTO FATWA!
WANTED DEAD (OR ALIVE) 25 MILLION BUCKS!

TROUBLETOWN

BY LLOYD DANGLE

DEPLOYMENT OF FOOD TO STARVING AFGHANI PEOPLE!

TUNA SANDWICH! I WAS EXPECTING SOMETHING ELSE.

U.S.A FANCY ALBACORE

WHOOMP!

BUSH'S TEAR: THE SHOCKING, UNSCRIPTED MOMENT THAT GAVE US HOPE.

GOD, NO!

LIVE TV

HE'S HUMAN!

BARBARA LEE'S VOTE: EVEN IF YOU'RE WITH THE 99.8%, IT PROVES WE'RE STILL A DEMOCRACY!

NAY!

YEA NAY
518 1

AMERICA TELLS FALWELL TO GO ☆#?@ HIMSELF!

TERRORISM WAS GOD'S WAY TO PUNISH GAYS!

BLOW IT OUT YOUR ASS!

EAT ME!

GOD

YOU SUCK!

BILL MAHER TELLS UNPOPULAR JOKES ON TV WITHOUT BEING IMPRISONED OR HAULED BEFORE A SENATE SUBCOMMITTEE!

HOW LONG HAS YOUR SHOW BEEN A PROPAGANDA TOOL FOR AL QAEDA, MR. MAHER?

THE FLAG: WAVING IT ISN'T EXCLUSIVELY FOR RIGHT-WINGERS ANYMORE!

HELP, I'm...LOSING ...MY...POWERS!

NO WAR

AME LOVE IT OR LEAV IT!

WAR, JUST WAR

PEACE

TROUBLETOWN

BY LLOYD DANGLE

WITH THE ECONOMY IN THE TOILET AND THE WORLD GRIPPED BY FEAR, WE DECIDED IT WAS A GOOD TIME TO BORROW MONEY AND GO TO EUROPE.

WE'RE AMERICANS — YOU'LL NEVER DAMPEN OUR SPIRITS!

TIES   CRABS   NEWS

IS IT SAFE TO FLY? **VERY!** YOU FACE A GREATER RISK OF BEING ACCIDENTALLY SHOT AT THE AIRPORT THAN YOU DO OF DYING ON A PLANE!

DÜSSELDORF   ZÜRICH

CHICAGO   MILANO

THE AIRLINES ARE VERY CAREFUL ABOUT RESTRICTING ALL KNIVES, BUT THEY GIVE YOU A SHARP METAL FORK WITH YOUR MEAL!

I SWEAR HE RECLINED RIGHT INTO IT!

AND YOU DON'T KNOW THE **MEANING** OF TERROR UNTIL YOU'VE TRIED DRIVING IN ITALY!

YIKES! THAT TRUCK JUST MISSED US BY CENTIMETERS!

WATCH OUT FOR THE OLD LADIES IN THE ROAD!

TABACCI

OKAY, SO MAYBE IT WAS A LITTLE IRRESPONSIBLE FOR A HIGH-PROFILE CARTOONALIST LIKE ME TO IGNORE THE NEWS FOR TWO WEEKS DURING SUCH TIMES...

ASSALTI AERIE AMERICANI VERSO I TALIBANI!   PIU DI GRAPPA PER FAVORE!

BUT NOW THAT I'M BACK, THERE'S SO MUCH CATCHING-UP TO DO! AND IF SOME MONEY DOESN'T START ROLLING-IN, I'm IN DEEP TROUBLE!

OH, VERY FUNNY! POWDERY SUBSTANCE INSTEAD OF CHECKS!

WHAT WILL WEEKLY NEWSPAPERS THINK OF NEXT?

SHAKE!   SHAKE!

TROUBLETOWN

PANIC MANAGEMENT TEAM

BY LLOYD DANGLE

PANIC! WE HAVE PRETTY CREDIBLE INFO THAT THERE MIGHT BE ANOTHER TERRORIST ATTACK TODAY!

DON'T WORRY, THAT GUY'S GOT WHAT WE CALL "SPORES IN HIS SHORTS."

HE'S FULL OF IT.

THE ANTHRAX IS GARDEN VARIETY — IF YOUR GARDEN HAS A DEAD COW IN IT.

DON'T WORRY.

FAIRLY SOLID RUMOR HAS IT THAT ANOTHER ATTEMPT WILL BE MADE IN THE NEXT 6 DAYS!

COME ON! THAT GUY IS JUST GRABBING SOME UNSUBSTANTIATED PANIC TO MAKE HIMSELF LOOK GOOD!

AND TAKE ATTENTION AWAY FROM ME.

LOOK, STATISTICALLY, MILLIONS OF PEOPLE DIE EVERY DAY OF **NATURAL CAUSES.** THAT'S WHAT YOU SHOULD REALLY WORRY ABOUT.

DON'T WORRY, I'VE HEARD FROM CREDIBLE SOURCES THAT JOHN WALSH AND RUDY GIULIANI ARE GOING TO TEAM UP ON TV!

HAVE YOU SEEN

WAIT! THAT ANTHRAX IS **MILITARY GRADE!** DON'T WORRY THOUGH, IT LOOKS LIKE IT'S FROM **OUR** MILITARY.

IF NOTHING TERRIBLE HAPPENS TODAY, YOU CAN ASSUME WE SUCCEEDED IN THWARTING A PLOT.

TROUBLETOWN

BY LLOYD DANGLE

I DON'T UNDERSTAND HOW A HUGE TAX CUT WILL FIGHT TERRORISM, DICK, BUT YOU HAVE MY SUPPORT!

DEMOCRATS DON'T NEED TO KNOW. IT'S SECRET.

BIPARTISANSHIP WAS IN FULL BLOOM AFTER 9-11, UNTIL SUDDENLY:

YOU WERE **WARNED** OF HIJACKINGS! WHY DIDN'T YOU SAY SO!

OH MY! SOMEBODY JUST HANDED ME THIS MEMO — ANOTHER ATTACK IS **IMMINENT!**

THAT'S A CHEESEBURGER WRAPPER. I SAW YOU TAKE IT OUT OF YOUR POCKET.

OF COURSE IT IS, DUMMY! I DON'T CARRY CLASSIFIED DOCUMENTS OPENLY!!

I'M VERY SKEPTICAL. I DEMAND THAT CONGRESS SEE THE FULL REPORT.

THAT WOULD BE A BAD IDEA. I MUST EAT IT!

NOW, THIS UNCONFIRMED KRISPY KREME DONUT WRAPPER JUST CAME, INDICATING THAT OSAMA HAS TARGETED THE HIGGELTY-PIGGELTY BRIDGE—

IN **MY** DISTRICT?!

I MUST ALARM MY PEOPLE!

THE TIMING OF QAEDA'S THREATS IS PURE EVIL, DICK.

YES, MR. PRESIDENT.

TROUBLETOWN

BY LLOYD DANGLE

Panel 1: AT A SECRET, SECURE LOCATION, DEEP INSIDE COAL MOUNTAIN, DICK CHENEY ASSEMBLES HIS ANTI-TERRORISM STIMULUS PACKAGE TASK FORCE.

WHO NEEDS A DRINK?

Panel 2: CONGRATULATIONS, GENTLEMEN. OUR $100 BILLION PACKAGE WILL SAVE THE U.S. ECONOMY AND FIGHT TERRORISM WORLDWIDE.

Panel 3: FOR SECURITY REASONS ALL TASK FORCE MEMBERS BEAR A STRIKING PHYSICAL RESEMBLANCE TO DICK CHENEY.

Panel 4: $600 MILLION WILL GO TO **ENTEX** TO DEVELOP DRILL RIGS THAT WON'T STIR UP ANTHRAX SPORES.

YES!

Panel 5: AS A FURTHER PRE-CAUTION, ALL TASK FORCE PARTICIPANTS ARE FROM TEXAS.

Panel 6: **PANHANDLE PETROLEUM** WILL GET $500 MILLION TO DEVELOP LESS FUEL-EFFICIENT CARS, SO THAT OSAMA BIN LADEN WILL RUN OUT OF GAS FASTER.

CLAP! CLAP! CLAP! CLAP!

Panel 7: $700 MILLION FOR **TEXERGY FOSSIL PRODUCTS** TO MAKE GAS PUMPS THAT CAN WITHSTAND A NUCLEAR ATTACK!

POP!

Panel 8: $500 MILLION WILL GO TO STAMP OUT SOLAR POWER AND LIGHT RAIL, KNOWN BIN LADEN TERROR CELLS!

RIGHT ON.

Panel 9: AND IF THAT'S NOT ENOUGH, REPEAL OF THE **ALTERNATIVE MINIMUM TAX** WILL HAVE AL QAEDA SHAKING!

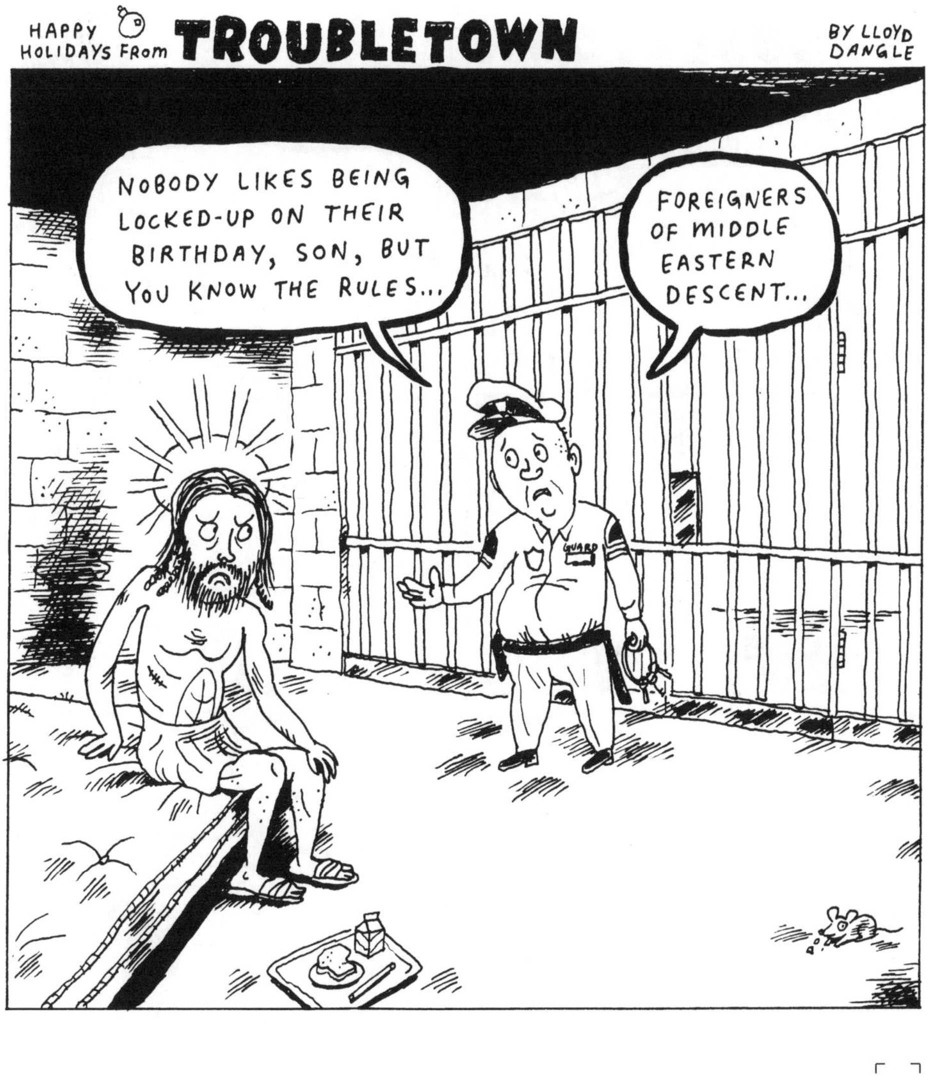
HAPPY HOLIDAYS FROM TROUBLETOWN
BY LLOYD DANGLE
NOBODY LIKES BEING LOCKED-UP ON THEIR BIRTHDAY, SON, BUT YOU KNOW THE RULES...
FOREIGNERS OF MIDDLE EASTERN DESCENT...
GUARD

TROUBLETOWN

BY LLOYD DANGLE

VICE PRESIDENT CHENEY IS ACCOSTED AT THE DOORWAY OF A REMOTE GOVERNMENT STEAM TUNNEL.

TOM DASCHLE! YOU SCARED THE CRAP OUTTA ME!

GOOD!

WHAT ARE YOU DOING HERE?

WHAT ARE **YOU** DOING HERE?

IF YOU MUST KNOW, I'M ON MY WAY TO MEET WITH THE SHADOW GOVERNMENT—AND CAN'T BE LATE!

WHY WASN'T I TOLD ABOUT THE SHADOW GOVERNMENT?

WE WERE WAITING FOR NEIL BUSH TO BE INSTALLED AS SHADOW PRESIDENT.

ARE THERE ANY DEMOCRATS IN THE SHADOW GOVERNMENT?

NO. THERE ARE MANY LEADERS FROM BUSINESS AND INDUSTRY, BUT THEY PROMISE TO **WORK** WITH DEMOCRATS!

YOU'RE TALKING ABOUT A GOVERNMENT MADE UP OF YOUR WEALTHY TEXAN CONTRIBUTORS!

PLEASE EXCUSE ME.

I DEMAND A LIST OF SHADOW GOVERNMENT MEMBERS!

THAT'S PROTECTED UNDER VEEP— WEALTHY TEXAN CONFIDENTIALITY!

TROUBLETOWN

BY LLOYD DANGLE

SO, NOW WE KNOW THAT THE FBI HAD THE CLUES, BUT THE ENTRENCHED BUREAUCRACY FAILED TO PREVENT THE CARNAGE OF SEPTEMBER 11.

NOW THAT THE UNTHINKABLE IS AS THINKABLE AS YOUR MORNING TOAST, THE CONCERN ISN'T SO MUCH ABOUT **ROGUE COPS,** BUT RATHER, ARE THEY **ROGUE ENOUGH?**

HERE WITH ME AT GROUND ZERO IS SOMEONE WHO KNOWS ABOUT STUPID POLICE BUREAUCRATS— CLINT EASTWOOD.

PLEASURE.

CLINT, WOULD YOU HAVE HANDLED THINGS DIFFERENTLY?

I WOULD'VE WALKED INTO FLIGHT SCHOOL BRANDISHING A .357, CHASED THE SCUMBAG ACROSS A RUNWAY, WOUNDED HIM, THEN STEPPED ON HIS NECK.

AFTER TORTURING THE PUNK FOR INFORMATION, I'D STEAL A PLANE, COLLIDE IT INTO FLIGHT 11, CRAWL ACROSS THE BURNING WING, SHOOT ALL THE TERRORISTS IN A BLOODY RAMPAGE, AND LAND BOTH PLANES SAFELY.

WOULD YOU HAVE GOTTEN A SEARCH WARRANT?

NO!

ON SEPTEMBER 11, FANTASY **BECAME** OUR REALITY! MAYBE WE NEED TO FACE REALITY BY HAVING THE COURAGE TO BELIEVE IN FANTASY LAW ENFORCEMENT.

TROUBLETOWN

BY LLOYD DANGLE

AT THE BIG GAME, HEIGHTENED SECURITY IS IN FULL EFFECT.

BAGS AND CARS ARE SEARCHED; BOMB SNIFFING DOGS ARE ON ALERT; THE SIX-BEERS-AT-A-TIME LIMIT IS STRICTLY EN-FORCED; BATHROOMS ARE CLOSED.

DUMP THE DESIGNER WATER, M'AM.

GATE 9

192 NEW SECURITY CAMERAS HAVE BEEN INSTALLED IN AND AROUND THE STADIUM TO FOLLOW PATRONS' EVERY MOVE.

NO URINATION

UH-OH.

SURE, THERE'LL ALWAYS BE SOME DORKS WHO SAY "BIG BROTHER IS WATCHING," BUT THE WORLD CHANGED FOREVER ON SEPTEMBER 11!

I GUESS, SINCE IT'S TO KEEP US SAFE, IT'S OKAY.

I'LL ACCEPT ANYTHING TO STOP OSAMA.

YOU MEAN I'M ON TV RIGHT NOW?!

KINGS

HI MOM

THANKFULLY NO TERRORISTS WERE FOUND THIS WEEKEND...

BUT A RECORD NUMBER OF ARRESTS WERE MADE FOR TICKET SCALPING, RUDENESS, MINOR DRUG OFFENSES, AND INDECENT EXPOSURE!

IT'S ALL GOOD!

TROUBLETOWN

OTHER PRE-EMPTIVE SOLUTIONS

BY LLOYD DANGLE

GIVE PILOTS GUNS.

PILOTS ONLY
☺
GUNS OKAY

GIVE MALL SECURITY GUARDS UNLIMITED SURVEILLANCE AUTHORITY.

VICTORIA'S SECRET
VICTORIA'S SECRET

ARM POSTAL EMPLOYEES WITH PRE-EMPTIVE ANTHRAX.

SNIFF THIS, FIDO,

US MAIL

GRR!

GIVE FLIGHT ATTENDANTS WIDE POISONING LATITUDE.

SPECIAL MEAL?

INFILTRATE SAUDI ARABIAN FUNDAMENTALIST SCHOOLS WITH BRITTANY SPEARS,

I'M SO CONFUSED!

PEPS

REQUIRE CONGRESS TO DESTROY ALL LETTERS FROM CONSTITUENTS WITHOUT READING THEM.

DUE TO 9/11, ALL BRIBES MUST BE HAND DELIVERED.

ENLIST THE NATION'S SUICIDAL.

YOU THINK YOU'VE GOT PROBLEMS!

EQUIP BUS DRIVERS WITH EJECTION SEATS.

I HEARD TWO CHILDREN SPEAKING PIG LATIN!

ZING!

LAIDLAW
STOP WHEN FLASHING
SCHOOL

ALLOW TALK SHOW FOREIGN AFFAIRS EXPERTS AND OTHER CELEBRITIES TO CARRY TINY NUCLEAR DEVICES.

I MAY HAVE TO TAKE OUT AL QAEDA IN BETWEEN MY LIMO AND THE GREEN ROOM.

TROUBLETOWN

BY LLOYD DANGLE

I THINK THE RULES AGAINST TORTURE AND ASSASSINATION ARE A LITTLE TOO STRICT.

WE CAN PROBABLY AFFORD TO LOSE SOME OF OUR FREEDOMS, I DON'T USE A LOT OF 'EM ANYWAY.

SURE, SOME THINGS MAY **NEED** TO BE CENSORED — LIKE IF THERE'S A CHANCE IT COULD CONTAIN SOME SECRET CODE!

I USED TO THINK RACIAL PROFILING WAS BAD, BUT NOW I DO IT ALL THE TIME! POLICE!

NO, I DON'T MIND. I **WANT** THE GOVERNMENT TO OPEN MY MAIL!

A LITTLE BIT OF RELIGIOUS INTOLERANCE IS OKAY AS LONG AS IT'S DONE WITH SENSITIVITY.

I'M NOT INTO PUBLIC BEATINGS AT ALL, BUT THESE ARE EXTRAORDINARY TIMES.

WOMEN SHOULDN'T BE ALLOWED TO LEAVE THEIR HOMES WITHOUT A MAN— TO PROTECT THEM FROM ANTHRAX!

YEAH, I CAN ACCEPT A CERTAIN LEVEL OF **TALIBANIZATION** IF IT WILL HELP.

TROUBLETOWN

BY LLOYD DANGLE

THE NATION'S AIRPORT BAGGAGE SCREENERS WERE INCOMPETENT SO THE FEDERAL GOVERNMENT HAD TO TAKE OVER.

WHAT AM I LOOKING FOR? HEH! HEH!

STEP ASIDE.

THE IMMIGRATION & NATURALIZATION SERVICE WAS INCOMPETENT SO THEY GOT **KICKED OUT** OF THE FEDERAL GOVERNMENT!

WHY DID I MAIL THAT VISA TO MOHAMMED ATTA?!

HEY, I'M A BAGGAGE AGENT. CAN I HAVE YOUR LOCKER?

THE FBI KEEPS ARRESTING THE WRONG PEOPLE AND SCREWING UP EVIDENCE. THEY MIGHT BE REPLACED BY PRIVATE GUMSHOES.

@#%☆ WEN HO LEE!

MOVE YER FEDERAL ASS— BEFORE I SLAP YOU.

THE NATIONAL GUARD IS UNABLE TO STOP PEOPLE AT AIRPORTS WHO CARRY GUNS, KNIVES, AND BOMBS. REPLACE THEM WITH SOLDIERS OF FORTUNE!

I'LL SELL THE URANIUM!

HOWDY.

THE COURT AND PRISON PUBLIC-PRIVATE PARTNERSHIP EXECUTES INNOCENT PEOPLE SOMETIMES. WHAT WILL REPLACE IT?

A FULLY AUTOMATED DNA DATABASE THAT INSTANTLY TERMINATES ANY PERPETRATOR!

THE ENRON CORPORATION WAS RIFE WITH CONSPIRACY AND CORRUPTION. THE PRESIDENT & CONGRESS SHOULD BE **FEDERALIZED** INSTEAD OF WORKING FOR THEM!

HUH?

THE GOVERNMENT ALREADY INTERFERES ENOUGH IN MY LIFE!

TROUBLETOWN

BY LLOYD DANGLE

TROUBLETOWN

BY LLOYD DANGLE

OKAY, WE ADMIT WE REALLY SCREWED UP!

WE DID.

WE WEREN'T **LISTENING** ENOUGH TO EACH OTHER!

WE NEED TO TALK MORE.

BUT NOW THAT WE DECIDED TO GIVE OUR-SELVES VAST NEW POWERS, WE'LL DO BETTER!

DON'T WORRY, IT WON'T BE A RETURN TO THE "BAD OLD DAYS."

NOBODY WANTS THAT!

WE'RE NOT GOING TO SURVEIL JUST ANYBODY!

UNLESS THEY MIGHT BE SUPPORTING TERRORISM.

WE'RE NOT GOING TO TOPPLE FOREIGN LEADERS WHOM WE DISLIKE,

UNLESS THE REASON WE DISLIKE THEM IS TERRORISM!

WE WON'T SPY ON WTO PROTESTORS, ENVIRON-MENTALISTS, OR PROPONENTS OF MEDICAL MARIJUANA.

UNLESS THEIR ACTIONS AID TERRORISTS.

MOST AMERICANS APPLAUD OUR NEW MEASURES. ALL EXCEPT FOR CIVIL LIBERTARIANS...

WHICH IS EXACTLY WHAT OSAMA WANTS!

THEY MIGHT AS WELL HAVE FLOWN THOSE PLANES THEMSELVES!

TRAITORS!

TROUBLETOWN

BY LLOYD DANGLE

HOW MANY TERRORISM SUSPECTS ARE BEING DETAINED?

BETWEEN 50 AND 5000. THE REAL NUMBER IS SECRET.

WHAT WILL HAPPEN TO THEM?

SOME OF THEM WILL BE TRIED IN SECRET, BY SECRET MILITARY TRIBUNALS.

WHAT TYPE OF EVIDENCE HAS BEEN FOUND?

SECRET EVIDENCE.

IS THE PRESIDENT SECRETLY EXPANDING THE WAR TO IRAQ?

IF I TOLD YOU, IT WOULDN'T BE A SECRET THEN, WOULD IT?

WILL HE CONSULT CONGRESS?

SECRETLY. UNLESS A SECRET EXECUTIVE ORDER BECOMES NECESSARY.

WILL ASHCROFT SEEK SECRET POWERS?

PLEASE! DON'T ASK ME TO TIP OUR HAND TO BIN LADEN!

WHO HAS ACCESS TO MILITARY ANTHRAX?

THAT'S FOR ME TO KNOW AND YOU TO FIND OUT.

CAN YOU GIVE US A HINT AS TO YOUR IDENTITY?

HOMELAND SECURITY DICTATES THAT I REMAIN ANONYMOUS.

HOW DO WE KNOW FOR SURE THAT Y-Y-YOU AREN'T A TERRORIST?

WATCH IT, PAL! THAT KIND OF CRAZY TALK CAN GET YOU INTO DEEP TROUBLE!

TROUBLE TOWN

BY LLOYD DANGLE

FINALLY, ONE MORE FORMALITY BEFORE WE BLOW IRAQ TO SMITHEREENS!

THE UN INSPECTORS ALL WEAR GLASSES AND LOOK NEAR-SIGHTED. WILL THEY BE EFFECTIVE? IT DOESN'T MATTER.

WHAT IF THEY DON'T FIND ANYTHING? IT'S EVIDENCE THAT SADDAM'S HIDING IT! WE'LL WIPE THE FLOOR WITH 'EM!

WHAT IF THEY **DO** FIND SOMETHING? EVIDENCE THAT SADDAM HAS BEEN LYING — WHICH WE ALREADY KNOW!

WE'LL BOMB THE CRAP OUT OF 'EM!

BECAUSE IF THEY FIND SOMETHING AND WE KNOW SADDAM IS LYING, IT **PROVES** THAT OTHER THINGS ARE BEING HIDDEN!

IT'S HIGHLY UNLIKELY THAT THE INSPECTORS WILL FIND **ALL** THE THINGS THAT ARE HIDDEN — REQUIRING US TO STOMP ASS!

HOW LONG WILL THEY HAVE TO FIND WEAPONS OF MASS DESTRUCTION? A MONTH. AFTER THAT THEY CAN GO HOME & LET UNCLE SAM MOP UP THE MESS.

MEANWHILE, AT THE UN: INSPECTING IRAQ IS EASY. CONTAINING A MASSIVELY DESTRUCTIVE SUPERPOWER WILL BE A BITCH!

ZAIRE   ZAIRE   NORW   CANADA

117

TROUBLETOWN

BY LLOYD DANGLE

A MILLION PEOPLE DEMONSTRATED IN ROME. IGNORE IT, THEY'RE ONLY CATHOLICS.

HANS BLIX SAYS THE SATELLITE PICTURES DON'T MEAN ANYTHING. IGNORE IT, THE UN IS IRRELEVANT!

100,000 PEOPLE DEMONSTRATED IN PARIS. IGNORE IT, *☆©# FROGS! FOCUS ON SADDAM.

GREENSPAN IS CRITICAL OF THE TAX CUT. IGNORE IT, FOCUS ON SADDAM!

200,000 PEOPLE DEMONSTRATED IN SAN FRANCISCO. IGNORE IT, ©☆%# FAGS! FOCUS ON SADDAM.

GREAT BRITAIN'S SPY INTELLIGENCE TURNED OUT TO BE A PLAGIARIZED GRAD STUDENT ESSAY; TWO MILLION DEMONSTRATED IN LONDON. SAD- DAM

OSAMA SENT ANOTHER TAPE! AMERICANS HAD A DUCT-TAPE-BUYING FRENZY! FOCUS THE FEAR ON THE FLIMSY SADDAM CONNECTION.

ALL IN ALL, THINGS ARE GOING WELL... WE HAVE 100% SUPPORT HERE ON **PLANET DUBYA!**

AND WE CAN COUNT ON OIL COMPANY CONSULTING GIGS FOR THE REST OF ALL TIME! FOSSIL-TEX EXPLORATION INC.

TROUBLETOWN

5:00 AM: EVERY DAY THE SAME DILEMMA PRESENTS ITSELF:

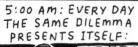

LOTT YEARNS FOR A STROM THURMOND PRESIDENCY! GORE REFUSES TO RUN.

I'M DEAD MEAT.

I'M DEAD WOOD.

KISSINGER QUITS TO PROTECT HIS BUSINESS CONTACTS!

BUSINESS CARDS

SKELETONS

CHENEY SPENDS TAX DOLLARS REMODELING "SECRET LOCATION."

I CAN'T CULTIVATE CONFLICTS OF INTEREST IN A DUMP!

MICHAEL JACKSON'S NOSE; THE OFFICE OF INFORMATION AWARENESS!

IRAQ WEAPONS INSPECTIONS; WINONA RYDER'S CONVICTION.

SADDAM COLLECTS LADIES' SHOES!

JFK WAS A SICK PUPPY; WHITNEY HOUSTON DENIES SMOKING CRACK.

OUCH! MY BACK!

DEMOCRATS LACK ANY PLAN OR VISION; DISNEY CRUISES GIVE GASTROINTESTINAL TRAUMA.

RALPH!

MISS WORLD PAGEANT CAUSES MUSLIM FATWA; PEDOPHILIA CAUSES CATHOLIC BROUHA.

WELCOME BACK, ADMIRAL POINDEXTER; WELCOME MEXICAN TRUCKERS!

BUENOS DIAS!

BUSH CARRIES HIS DOG EVERWHERE; CONSUMERS REFUSE TO SPEND; NORTH KOREA HAS A NUCLEAR BOMB...

THERE'S **TOO MUCH** MATERIAL! HOW WILL I EVER CATCH UP?

ABOUT
THE AUTHOR

Lloyd Dangle has been writing and drawing Troubletown
cartoons for alternative newsweeklies since 1988. His
comics and illustrations have appeared elsewhere in
over one-hundred publications of every conceivable
type, from the crusty corporate mainstream to the
bleeding subcommercial edge.

Dangle lives in Oakland, California, where he coasts into
his mid-40's, sheltered and protected from stress and
pain by his wealthy and beautiful wife, Hae Yuon Kim,
and their son, Oscar.

Other books and comics by Lloyd Dangle:
> ***Troubletown***
> ***Second Hand and Previously-Used Troubletown***
> ***Contract with Troubletown***
> ***Next Stop: Troubletown***
> ***Focus Group Tested Troubletown***
> ***Troubletown Funky Hipster Trash***
> ***Troubletown Manifestos 'n' Stuff***
> ***Real Recipes for Comic Cooks*** (with Lynn Gordon)
> ***Dangle*** (comic book series)

Available at:
www.troubletown.com

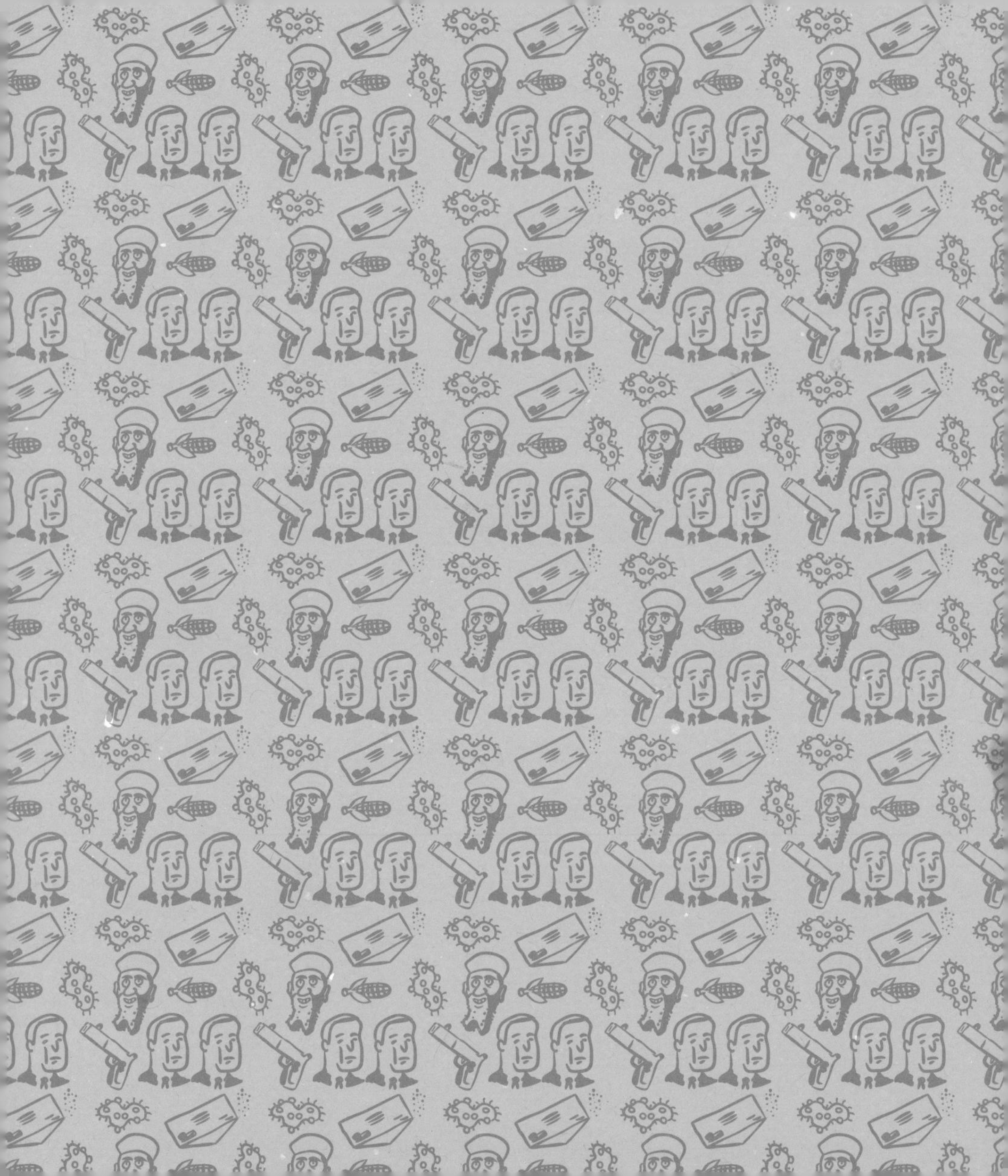